THE SPIRIT OF '76

OTHER BOOKS BY CARL BRIDENBAUGH
BEARING ON THE AMERICAN REVOLUTION

SILAS DOWNER, FORGOTTEN PATRIOT:
His Life and Writings

CITIES IN REVOLT:
Urban Life in America, 1743–1776

THE COLONIAL CRAFTSMAN

MITRE AND SCEPTRE:
*Transatlantic Faiths, Ideas, Personalities, and
Politics, 1689–1775*

REBELS AND GENTLEMEN:
Philadelphia in the Age of Franklin
(Co-author)

PETER HARRISON:
First American Architect

SEAT OF EMPIRE:
The Political Role of Eighteenth-Century Williamsburg

MYTHS AND REALITIES:
Societies of the Colonial South

A TOUR THROUGH PART OF THE NORTH
PROVINCES OF AMERICA
By Patrick M'Robert, 1776
(Edited, with an introduction)

THE
SPIRIT OF
'76

The Growth of American Patriotism
Before Independence 1607—1776

Carl Bridenbaugh

OXFORD UNIVERSITY PRESS

London   Oxford   New York

OXFORD UNIVERSITY PRESS

London   Oxford   New York
Glasgow   Toronto   Melbourne   Wellington
Cape Town   Ibadan   Nairobi   Dar es Salaam   Lusaka   Addis Ababa
Delhi   Bombay   Calcutta   Madras   Karachi   Lahore   Dacca
Kuala Lumpur   Singapore   Hong Kong   Tokyo

To
Whitfield J. Bell and *Edwin Wolf 2nd*
of Philadelphia

Preface

The following chapters on the genesis of the American spirit are not offered as a definitive treatment of the subject. My hope is rather to provide the bicentennial audience with an introduction to a strangely neglected aspect of our history from 1607 to 1776, which ought eventually to be chronicled by a number of historians in several volumes.

After reading, researching, and reflecting on the American Revolution for nearly half a century, I have not found in any of the many helpful explanations of this profoundly significant historical phenomenon what the rank and file of the colonists were really like in 1776 or what were their hopes, fears, and kindred emotions. One concludes that public issues alone never seemed sufficient cause for the curious combination of exuberance and resentment back of the revolt. There is always a social atmosphere, seldom recorded clearly in the documents, which a historian ordinarily handles, that largely molds events.

Any attempt by the historian to peer into the minds of men long dead can meet with but a partial success. First to sense, then to glimpse, and finally to represent for his readers a mood, a temper, or to gauge collective sentiments, is to describe the indescribable. Furthermore, as Edward Eggleston observed in 1900, "men may live in the same time without being intellectual contemporaries." Nevertheless, the effort should be made despite the difficulties of the task.

Whatever men's politics, whatever their religious affiliations, whatever their educations, whatever their cultural attainments, whatever their degrees of wealth or rank in society—and differences among them were many, varied, and highly complex—they all shared in a common love of the land in which they lived. Moreover, very early they recognized themselves as a new and markedly different breed of men from their European contemporaries. They knew that they were Americans and were proud of the distinction. It is this psychological attitude or spirit that will concern us.

In this venture at assessing the feelings and sentiments of the colonial public, I have relied heavily upon what these Americans said—both privately and openly—in the conviction that they were fully aware of what they were saying, and they meant what they said. Some of them exaggerated, others understated their positions, but we have no reason to brand them hypocrites, deceivers, or prevaricators. Surely John Adams was sincere and measured his words with care when he wrote in 1765: "I have always considered the settlement of America with reverence and wonder. . . ." Similarly, William Livingston was voicing not his private view but the popular confidence in the growing strength of America and its magnificent destiny with divine assistance when he warned Great Britain in 1768 that "There is no contending with Omnipotence." Many a Tory or loyalist felt much as Adams and Livingston did but differed radically about ways and means of achieving and enjoying American greatness.

The focus of this history is upon the growth of patriotism and republicanism of a peculiarly American kind. The formation of our national spirit must be described in American, not European, terms. Its religious aspects, therefore, claim much space. On the other hand, *equality* and *democracy*—both themes of great importance—are treated largely by implication. Each of them requires a separate volume.

Providence   Carl Bridenbaugh
1 October 1974

Acknowledgments

My heavy obligations for aid and assistance, always generously forthcoming over more than four decades, are of two distinct kinds:

First, this book originated in two lectures for my courses on Colonial History and The American Revolution, and I am beholden to many generations of students, both undergraduate and graduate, at the University of California, Berkeley, and Brown University, who listened patiently while I thought out my ideas before them and who, on occasion, made me defend them. In many ways David Corkran, Hunter Dupree, Albert Klyberg, and Richard Showman gave me helpful advice and moral support. Roberta Bridenbaugh's contribution to the volume, as always, is incalculable.

Second, a succession of kindly and patient librarians and archivists made it possible for me in the days before microfilm and microprint to read the newspapers in their custody at the Charleston Library Society, the Historical Society of Pennsylvania, the Library of Congress, and the New-York Historical Society. In this connection, my debt to the Massachusetts Historical Society is greatest and of longest duration. Most of the pamphlets and colonial sermons and tracts cited in the following pages are to be found in the John Carter Brown Library in Providence, where Jeannette Black and Samuel Hough have helped me immeasurably.

Readers familiar with the literature of the Colonial Period and the American Revolution will recognize at once that although I cite only the sources of my quotations and rare facts, I have profited from reading—and rereading—the classic and more recent secondary works on these subjects.

C.B.

Contents

THE SPIRIT OF '76

THE SPIRIT OF

Introduction

Patrick Henry rose in his place at the Carpenters' Hall in Philadelphia on September 6, 1774, to open the memorable debate of the First Continental Congress. "The Distinctions between Virginians, Pensylvanians, New Yorkers and New Englanders, are no more," he declaimed with moving eloquence. "I am not a Virginian, but an American." Little more than three weeks later, in proposing a plan for a continental legislature, Joseph Galloway of Pennsylvania advanced an opposite view: "I know of no American Constitution. A Virginia Constitution, A Pensylvanian Constitution We have. We are totally independent of each other." [1]

For the most part, posterity has dismissed Henry's assertion as hyperbole or mere windy oratory. Historians have tended to accept Galloway's position without making the distinction that was clear to John Adams and many others at the time: the Virginia patriot was alluding to the sentiments of the large and ever-increasing number of people who were distributed all the way from

1. *Diary and Autobiography of John Adams*, ed. L. H. Butterfield (Cambridge, 1961), II, 125, 126, 143.

Falmouth in Maine to Savannah in Georgia, whereas the future Tory leader was speaking about government and political institutions.

Sweeping legalism and logic aside, Patrick Henry expressed dramatically in two short sentences a demonstrable truth: there had burgeoned among colonists of all ranks a consciousness of intercolonial unity that may properly be called Americanism. If this belief in a common cause had not been a part of the feelings and thoughts of a substantial segment of the people, the outbreak of the revolt against Britain in 1774 would be inexplicable.

The failure to recognize this shift in public opinion has permitted the emergence, growth, and persistence of two misleading assumptions that have almost totally obscured the real nature of our history from 1763 to 1789. These misconceptions have long since been accepted as axiomatic and are incorporated in most textbooks of American history. If American history—which is the national memory—is not to remain distorted, these misreadings of the past must be corrected, the ideas inherent in them revised, and the public informed of the truth about this fundamental yet neglected phase of the nation's past.

What are the specific fallacies in these two misconceptions?

The clue to that in the first is discovered in a query and answer made in the Congress by Richard Henry Lee on September 28, 1774. "How did We go on for 160 Years before the Year 1763? We flourished and grew." Though his arithmetic was imprecise, the Virginian rightly assumed that his fellow members would understand what he had in mind.[2]

Dates repel modern school children, college students,

2. Adams, *Diary*, II, 143.

many writers, and most readers, but by following the lead of Colonel Lee, one can quickly see that the use of simple chronology places the American Revolution and the War for Independence in their necessary and proper perspective.

In 1607 the first permanent English settlement on this continent was made at Jamestown in Virginia. The span of time from 1607 to 1763, when the quarrel with Great Britain began, was *156 years;* from 1607 to 1776, the date of the Declaration of Independence, was *169 years;* and from 1607 to 1789, the year of establishing the government under the Constitution, it was *182 years.* A comparison of these periods with the passage of time since the Revolutionary Era is instructive: it has been *200 years* from 1776 to the present bicentennial; from 1783 it is *193 years;* and from the establishing of the present government, *187 years.*

This chronology demonstrates strikingly that if the year of the Declaration of Independence is to be used, the span of time since 1776 measures only *31 years* more than the period elapsing between 1607 and 1776. To put it briefly, *the colonial period is almost one half of all American history.* Many families of 1776 had lived in America for three, four, five, and some even six, generations. During the more than a century and a half in which they had lived in this land, about which clustered considerable tradition and history, they had come to love it as their own.

It is the obligation of anyone who would understand the complexity of what happened between 1763 and 1789 to keep this incontrovertible fact of the passage of time constantly in mind: THE AMERICAN REVOLUTION OCCURRED NOT AT THE BEGINNING BUT IN THE MIDDLE OF AMERICAN HISTORY.

The second misconception stems directly from the ne-

glect of chronology—of the factor of time. Taking 1776
or 1789 as their starting points for the study of American
nationalism rather than 1607, 1620, or 1630, many
writers have sought to trace an artificial growth by looking for elements resembling the nationalism of nine-
teenth-century Europe. D. H. Lawrence asserted that
the Americans did not fit into the classic pattern:
"America has never been a blood-home-land. Only an
ideal home-land. The home-land of the idea, of the *spirit*.
And of the pocket. Not of the blood." In *American Nationalism: An Interpretive Essay* (1957), the late Hans Kohn
declared that because they are not a folk, a people unified
linguistically and traditionally, the Americans do not
conform to the accepted rules about nationalism. Above
all, he maintained, they have no myths. It is not enough
to dismiss the distinguished English novelist and critic,
the learned immigrant from the Austro-Hungarian Empire, or several native-born writers on the subject with
Lin Yutang's pungent comment that "much scholarship
is merely learned nonsense." The only satisfaction can
come from a serious examination of the origin and
growth of feelings, or spirit, and opinions among the
people of the thirteen colonies during the half of American history that occurred before, not after, the year of
the Declaration of Independence.[3]

The object of the present bicentennial celebration is to
commemorate the Declaration of Independence. This is
both fitting and proper. But to the citizenry and, apparently, to most publicists and historians, the anniver-
sary is being directed even more to marking the birth of
the Republic and, by extension, the first fumbling efforts
to arouse the sense of unity that was so essential to

3. D. H. Lawrence, as quoted in *The Times Literary Supplement*,
   August 16, 1957, iii; Hans Kohn, *American Nationalism: An Interpretive Essay* (New York, 1957), 1–38.

counter the love of locality and provincial particularism. In this little book, however, the purpose of the author is to trace the rise and development of the sense of American unity that made the Declaration of Independence possible in 1776.

I
The Sweetness of the Country
1607-1690

Nationalism, a complex mixture of sentiments and loyalties, takes a very long time to form in the hearts and minds of a people and still longer before it can be outwardly displayed and clearly articulated. One would not ordinarily expect to uncover any evidence of a commonly shared sense of American destiny among many English colonists in the New World before 1690. Historians, as a rule, have emphasized the *Englishness* of the settlers and pictured them as complete colonials striving to live and have their daily being in as English a way as possible.

Upon closer examination of the record, however, it becomes quite clear that the slightly more than eight decades beginning in 1607 constituted the long period of gestation necessary for the later growth of an American spirit. It was during these years that English immigrants, plus a few Dutch, Swedes, Finns, and French Huguenots, seated themselves in the wilderness, learned how to live in the strange new environment, and began to think of the colonies as home. In the oldest settlements of 1690 lived many individuals of the second and third generations who knew no other homeland.

Nowhere on the continent of North America could accepted conditions for a European species of nationalism have been discovered. On the other hand, everywhere from the Penobscot to the Savannah rivers, the classic set of native conditions for producing new kinds of societies existed in profusion. By the very nature of things, these conditions fell into two categories.

The first was the natural environment. North America was separated from the British Isles by three thousand miles of restless ocean, whose expanse, at the outset of colonization, interposed a barrier of time-distance and ensured isolation from the mother country. This situation alone guaranteed that eventually the two would grow apart.

Once the emigrants had made the Atlantic crossing, the sheer extent and vastness of North America both dismayed and challenged them and forced them to revise many long-cherished ideas and practices. Distances were formidable rather than magnificent, and purple mountain majesties loomed as forbidding obstacles. To a rural or pastoral people the unanticipated presence of the apparently endless, dense, towering forest with its many dangerous species of wild animals threatened their very survival until, after a harsh apprenticeship, they learned how to become woodsmen and hunters. Wide rivers, such as the Kennebec, Connecticut, Hudson, and Delaware, or the great bay of Chesapeake, impeded travel and communication at the same time that they furthered transportation and trade.

Whether the English located themselves in the Chesapeake region or in New England, the climate differed noticeably from that to which they had been accustomed. Everywhere the extremes of heat and cold surprised them and required changes of clothing for which they were unprepared.

The prime attraction of America for most newcomers had been land, either cheap or free, but once a man had acquired a few acres, he had to clear them, break the ground, fence in his fields, and build a house. For none of these essential tasks was the ordinary farmer or artisan trained or hardened, but they did involve experiences common to the colonists wherever they settled.

An added situation shared by all of the first settlers was the pressing need to learn how to deal with the Indians. Friendly at first, the natives helped the settlers to survive by teaching them their agricultural lore and also how to fish and hunt; much of the meat consumed in the early years was brought in by Indian hunters. The natives also showed them the paths through the forest and how to fashion canoes; their wigwams gave the Europeans ideas for raising temporary shelters. But in time the white man's encroachments on the Red Man's lands and his often ruthless behavior antagonized and frightened the natives and inevitably brought about conflict. Accounts of the massacres of 1622 and 1644, and Bacon's Indian war of 1675 in Virginia, and the New England war with the Pequots, 1637, and later tales of King Philip's War, 1675–76, spread up and down the coast and made the English aware that defense against the Indians was a common problem.

The second category of the classic mode of American development is found in the people. Although the population, composed of transplanted Europeans, was overwhelmingly English before 1690, it was never truly representative of society in Britain. Almost no members of the nobility crossed the Atlantic to make new homes for themselves—"Dukes don't emigrate." Furthermore, a selective process operated in the migration of the lesser gentry, middle, and lower orders. For a variety of reasons, most of the men who went or were sent out to

America were disenchanted with things at home; they were vexed and troubled Englishmen. Some of them departed of their own volition; others—desperate men, criminals, paupers, or shanghaied men and women—left unwillingly. It is difficult to find evidence of men's thoughts, but thousands of people sailed westward entertaining little hope of bettering themselves, and in most cases their worst forebodings were borne out.

This was an age of intense religious convictions that suffused every department of existence. One thing that bound nearly all English emigrants together was that they were all Protestants. They hated Roman Catholics, notably their French and Spanish neighbors in the New World. Religious discontent had impelled great numbers of Puritans to seek freedom of worship according to their own lights in the New World. Although they could not conscientiously conform to the requirements of the Church of England, they officially denied that they were forsaking the state church; they were merely separating from its popish excrescences. However, when they arrived in New England in 1630 they worked out an ecclesiastical system that closely resembled the separatism of the Pilgrims, who had seated themselves at Plymouth in 1620. Insofar as religion figured in Virginia in those early days, the bulk of the indentured servants seem to have been indifferent; and the church-going planters, who belonged to the left-wing or low-church Anglicans, promptly by-passed the canons and altered procedures to fit local conditions. Maryland became a refuge in 1634 for Lord Baltimore's fellow Roman Catholics and soon, too, for a more numerous body of harassed Puritans from Virginia. Years later, in 1657, members of the Society of Friends led by George Fox settled on the Eastern Shore, and they spread from Accomac County in Virginia northward into Maryland; ultimately they extended their remarkably organized meetings all the way from Charleston to Portsmouth on the Piscataqua.

Throughout the colonies before 1690, active dissent from, rather than conformity to, the Church of England rooted itself and grew luxuriantly. When, after a century of neglect, concerned Anglicans attempted to strengthen their communion overseas, it was too late.

In England itself, though the speech of the Thames Valley—the King's English—was making headway against strong local dialects, accelerated no doubt by the mingling of Englishmen during the Civil Wars, many Britons still spoke dialects. A Cornishman could rarely understand the speech of a Yorkshireman. In the colonies, dialects at first interfered with general communication, but as the second and third generations came upon the scene, spoken English tended toward the uniformity that so surprised many foreign visitors in the next century. Already, too, the colonists were adopting many Indian and some Spanish, Dutch, and French words, which served to make their language diverge noticeably from the King's English.

In the last two decades of this period, there began a major change in the national and racial composition of the colonial population that would in time produce a society of many white nationalities and two races, African blacks and European whites. This new society would be drastically different from that of England, and the effects that this development would have upon English law and inherited traditions and customs can well be imagined.

Little by little during the course of the eight decades of colonial growth, the struggles for survival in the wilderness were being won. Though the battles may have seemed long and arduous to those involved, the pace of life and rate of change in the new settlements compared with those of contemporary Europe were unexpectedly rapid. The American process of progressively turning portions of the forest into productive farms had been going on steadily despite stubborn resistance frequently offered by the Indians, the Spanish, or the French. In areas where in 1600 there had been no permanent settlements of white men, in 1690 there was a population approaching 225,000. Community life was well established in a number of places, some of which had grown into sizable towns, such as Boston, Philadelphia, and New York. Successful adjustment, adaptation, improvisation, even invention, were what produced this startling accomplishment.

The most arresting and important aspect of this transformation of the wilderness into a settled countryside was that it simultaneously produced in the colonial people a metamorphosis that varied according to region. Everywhere the inhabitants of the colonies were becoming less and less English than they had been any time before 1650. Without this silent but positive growth during the seventeenth century, the astonishing dynamic colonial expansion and development of the eighteenth could never have occurred.

The founding of New England by Puritans, Separatists, and other dissenters from the established Anglican church had led by 1690 to the settling of the colonies of New Hampshire, Massachusetts, Plymouth, Rhode Island and Providence Plantations, and Connecticut, plus the Yankee plantations of eastern Long Island. The inhabitants of all these areas, taken together, composed a single cohesive and rapidly maturing society exhibiting distinctive regional traits. The history of the past five centuries does not record—if indeed it ever had previously—a colonial enterprise as successful as the one that certain of the English Puritans undertook of their own volition in New England.

Governor William Bradford reported to Robert Cushman in England on June 9, 1625, that the settlers at Plymouth "never felt the sweetness of the country till this year; and not only we but all planters in the land begin to do it." Just as quickly, too, most of the Puritans who followed the Pilgrims into the new Canaan by the thousands between 1629 and 1642 savored existence in their new homeland. Writing in his *Memoirs* of arriving at Dorchester in 1630, Roger Clap told how God had given him "Contentedness in all these straits," and that "I do not remember that ever I did wish in my Heart that I had not come into this Country, or wish myself back again to my Father's House. . . . And then there was great Love one to another; very ready to help each other; not seeking their own, but every one another's Wealth." [1]

So quickly did the founding of new settlements and towns proceed that by 1642 Edward Johnson could describe it as "indeed the wonder of the world." What really impressed him was the well-being of the people: "There are not many Towns in the Country, but the poorest person in them hath a house and land of his own, and bread of his own growing, if not some cattel; beside, flesh is now no rare food, beef, pork, and mutton being frequent in many houses, so that this poor Wilderness hath not only equalized England in food, but goes beyond it in some places for the great plenty of wine and

1. William Bradford, "Letter Book," Massachusetts Historical Society, *Collections*, III, 36–37; *Memoirs of Roger Clap*, ed. Thomas Prince (Boston, 1731), 4, 13.

sugar . . . and now, good white and wheaten bread is not dainty, but even an ordinary man hath his choice." [2]

Other observers readily recognized the steadily improving and widespread well-being of the colonists in New England. At London in 1656, the Lord Protector conceded the soundness of the objections by one of his old officers, John Leverett, then an agent for the Bay Colony, to his pet scheme for recruiting a large company of New England Puritans to go to tropical Jamaica and improve their condition. "As to the bettering of our outward condition," Leverett wrote back to the General Court, "though we had not many among us that had to boast, as some particulars in other plantations, of raising themselves to great estates, yet take the body of the people and all things considered, they lived more comfortably like Englishmen than any of the rest of the plantations . . . to which I added, that *there were more in New-England produced to bespeak us a commonwealth* than in all the English plantations besides, the which His Highness granted." [3]

When John Leverett labeled New England a commonwealth, he had in mind Massachusetts—the names were then used interchangeably. But the survey of the entire area made in 1660 by one who had lived there the longest and was the most traveled and best informed resident, Samuel Maverick, provided a comprehensive description of settlement extending from Pemaquid southward and westward as far as the river Delaware, "the utmost Southwest bounds of New England." Despite his reputation as one of the most influential critics of the Pu-

2. *Johnson's Wonder-Working Providence, 1628–1651,* ed. J. Franklin Jameson, Original Narratives of Early American History (New York, 1952), 210.

3. Thomas Hutchinson, *History of the Colony and Province of Massachusetts-Bay,* ed. Lawrence S. Mayo (Cambridge, 1936), I, 163*n.* (italics mine).

ritan regime and an advocate of revoking the Massachusetts charter, Maverick, in an honest and factual account, presented irrefutable evidence of a prosperous people, many towns, "handsome Houses and Churches," and thriving agriculture and commerce, which even he admitted to being "a wonder." [4]

Nowhere else in the mid-seventeenth century could one find communities where a large majority of the rank and file of men, women, and children fared so well. The New Englanders were, indeed, most fortunate. The freemen of Charlestown actually stated officially in 1668 that "for many yeares" they had been "the most happy people that wee know of in the world." [5]

Expressions of public contentment and satisfaction, as well as of burgeoning local pride, continued to mount with the coming of age of the third generation of New Englanders. Cotton Mather labeled the native-born "Criolians," but the world knows them as Yankees, a breed that appeared after 1660 and that could be readily distinguished from the basic English stock by 1690. The Reverend Mr. Mather preached in *A Pillar of Gratitude* sentiments about his native soil that, however much they may arouse smiles today, expressed vividly and precisely the attitudes of his Yankee auditory and readers: "And tho' it be not The Glory of all Lands, yet Englishmen could not have met with many better Lands. Deservedly it is called New England; for England, that bravest Lady of Europe, has no where in America a Daughter that so much Resembles her. The Comforts of the Climate

---

4. Samuel Maverick, A Briefe Discription of New England and the Severall Touns therein, together with the Present Government thereof [1660], British Museum: Egerton MSS, 2395, fols. 399–411; also printed in Massachusetts Historical Society, *Proceedings*, 2d series, I, 231–49.
5. Charlestown Petition, Massachusetts Archives (State House, Boston), LXVII, 51.

abundantly outweigh the Hardship of it. The Poor find a
more comfortable Subsistence in it, than almost any
other. Almost every where else the Poor do rather En-
dure Life, than enjoy it . . . And where the Inhabitants
of it use Discretion and Industry, they mostly furnish
themselves, not only with Necessaries, but also with
Conveniencies. *Indeed New England is not Heaven: But for
my part, I do not ask to Remove out of New-England, except for
a Removal into Heaven.*" [6]

This ringing declaration by a leader of the third generation goes far beyond mere appreciation of the sweetness
of the land or even a surging pride of locality; it is an
open profession of a deep provincial patriotism that circulated like smoke not only over Massachusetts but over
all of the five New England colonies. Moreover, this
unity of the colonists about their region was unique.
How did it come about?

One can discover the secret of New England in the
people who settled it and in the powerful religious impulse known as Puritanism. As he was preparing to lead
the migration from England, John Winthrop observed
significantly that former colonial ventures, especially that
of the Virginia Company, had failed principally because
"their mayne end was Carnall and not Religious" and
"they used unfitt instrumentes, a multitude of rude and
misgovernd persons, the very scumme of the Land." The
Puritans firmly believed that God was actively urging
them to seek out a new country in which they were to

6. "As they tell me, That the Peasants of the other Countreiyes are
meer Bruits to what they are in England: I suppose Ours are not
worse than Englands. Yea, I have heard unprejudiced strangers
own, That there is yet left proportionately more Piety in this
Land, and the Common people are for the most part, better instructed, than in any they know of under Heaven." Cotton
Mather, *A Pillar of Gratitude* (Boston, 1700), 10–11, 22 (italics mine).

create a new society under His direction and with His blessing. They pictured themselves as the modern Israelites crossing to the promised land. As early as 1642 the moderate Anglican, Thomas Fuller, curate of the Savoy, was able to write: "I am confident, that America, though the youngest sister of the four [continents], is now grown marriageable, and daily hopes to get Christ to her Husband, by the preaching of the Gospel." [7]

Assurances through preaching and private prayers, not only of God's presence but of His guidance of every event or mere happening, no matter how trivial, enabled the Puritans to accept with resignation all occurrences good or bad as being divinely ordained. Although constantly searching for evidence that he himself was one of the elect who would be saved, the Puritan recognized that God had called him to work hard and to prosper in this life. Worldly success was the badge of divine approval; idleness was a cardinal sin.

The founding of the new colony of Massachusetts was carefully planned well in advance of the migration and adequately financed and widely advertised by an unusually able, experienced, and practical, as well as wholly committed, group of merchants, country gentlemen, and ministers. They envisaged their Puritan followers making permanent homes and building godly communities. The society would be, proclaimed John Winthrop, as a city on a hill and a beacon light to the rest of the Christian world. Unlike the get-rich-quick projectors of the day, the leaders did not propose to sell off their land in parcels; rather they would give it away free of feudal encumbrances to each right-thinking freeman that he and his family might enjoy farming and living upon it. Their settlement was to be godly and an agricultural Utopia.

7. *Winthrop Papers* (Boston, 1931), II, 143; Thomas Fuller, *The Holy and the Profane State*, ed. James Nichols (London, 1841), 185.

"Wee must be knitt together in this worke as one man," said Winthrop aboard the *Arbella* in 1630, "allwayes haveing before our eyes our Commission and Community in the worke, our Community as members of the same body, soe shall wee keepe the unitie of the spirit in the bond of peace. . . ." [8]

The success of such a holy experiment depended first and last upon the quality of the ordinary people who ventured everything they owned and prized in it. The ablest of leaders could never have carried out the best of plans without the rank and file "Souldiers of Christ," as Edward Johnson called them. The opportunity to enjoy "liberties of worship" denied them in England, to cultivate lands of their own, and to prosper in the Lord's service attracted thousands of solid and "godly" Puritans and their families to join in the movement. No English colony in the Chesapeake area or the West Indies started out with the family as its fundamental unit or represented so nearly an actual cross section of the society of Britain with respect to sex and age. They were also a picked lot. Surveying the undertaking years later in 1666, William Stoughton, who had arrived very early in the migration, explained the selection process: "God sifted a whole nation that he might bring choice Grain over into this Wildernesse." [9]

The striking cohesiveness of the society of early New England stemmed from the fundamental fact that it was the product of a group migration of like-minded people. In more than a few instances, ministers were accompanied into exile by numbers of their English parishioners; more often bands of Puritans from a single town or from one area sailed together to establish themselves in

8. *Winthrop Papers*, II, 294, 295.
9. William Stoughton, *New Englands True Interest Not to Lie* (Boston, 1670), 19.

the New World. The number who went involuntarily
was negligible. Above all else, this was a family hegira in
which husbands and wives with their children and
household servants emigrated willingly, freely, and hope-
fully for the most part rather than as laborers under individual contracts or by enticement, force, or misrepre-
sentation as did so many of the youthful emigrants who
left in the same years for the Caribbean or Chesapeake
Bay colonies. From documents since lost, Thomas
Hutchinson learned that the 21,200 settlers of New
England made up "about 4000 families." [10]

Although the professed goal of the first colonists had
been to attain a state of godliness, the Puritans lived and
died in the midst of life, confident that God wanted them
to live and die that way. Sustained in every crisis, personal or community, by an unshakable faith that the
Lord was on their side and that whatever happened was
dictated by His inscrutable will, they managed individ-
ually and collectively to make an unprecedented accommodation with their harsh surroundings. The frequent
juxtaposing of increasing individuality and the binding
requirements of "a well ordered society" can be either a
good or a bad thing, but for the men and women of that
era it must have proved exciting to observe and experience it. Social tensions so obsess many historians today
as to divert them from recognizing the profound truth
that though the New Englanders experienced tensions in
great plenty—plus the awful fear for their own souls,
which no longer agitates us moderns—still, in the end,
those colonists appear to have silently conceded that
whatever was best for the town, the church, and the
common weal was also best for the individual.

During the first years, the great body of the Puritans

10. Hutchinson, *History*, I, 82.

had to adjust themselves, their habits, notions, and ideas to new kinds of housing, husbandry, and industrial pursuits merely to survive and worship in New England. Concurrently they were forced to adapt themselves to strange climatic and physical conditions, to sudden social changes, sometimes to novel political institutions and different cultural attitudes, to shifting manners and unfamiliar moral standards, and to new psychological imperatives and altered superstitions. In addition they had to accustom themselves to treating puzzling ailments and practicing odd ways of maintaining health, as well as to eating curious foods—even socially undesirable and radical persons, like ordinary conforming townsfolk, clung to the fondly remembered diet of their native place, as do emigrants in all ages. Knowingly or unconsciously, the New England Puritans made major and minor concessions in all avenues of life: failures were relatively few, and by 1660 they had effected an almost complete adaptation. The essential Yankee mood was to make a virtue out of necessity by means of unremitting toil.

The process of adaptation commenced with the Atlantic crossing, which forced these insular Englishmen to revise their notions of distance. Inexperienced as they were at pioneering, once they went ashore they had to erect temporary shelters or dig them in the ground and, as soon as possible, to build more permanent dwellings. Sooner or later they had to learn how to fell trees, clear out underbrush, and break up the stubborn, stony soil. Then the traditional lore of English farming had either to be altered markedly or abandoned, and such strange Indian crops as maize, squashes, pumpkins, and beans planted and cultivated. The harsh winters dictated a much different animal husbandry than that brought over from Essex and Kent. And before too long, when time permitted, they built meetinghouses, barns, outbuildings, warehouses, as well as wharves and fences.

Faced with more than 22,000 inhabitants, it was necessary for the authorities of Massachusetts in 1640 to permit migrations to Connecticut, New Hampshire, and Rhode Island where large areas of richer intervale lands existed. Small agricultural surpluses became available by the end of the forties, and Plymouth benefited by supplying grain and livestock to the towns of the Bay. Connecticut shippers were dispatching quantities of produce to Boston and exporting increasing amounts to Barbados and St. Christopher. Meanwhile the refugees from Puritan intolerance and persecution successfully developed a lucrative grazing industry on the islands of Narragansett Bay. As Sir Henry Moody would shortly explain, in Rhode Island "there is enough of 2 good things, Fat Mutton and Liberty of Conscience." [11]

Although the founders had intended to develop New England as an exclusively agricultural society, they turned to the sea very early in order to supplement the meager crops of Massachusetts. Fishing, then coastal shipping, and eventually distant ocean commerce to the Wine Islands, West Indies, and Europe led to the growth of classes of merchants and artisans and the rise of Boston as the metropolis of the English colonies. Portsmouth, Salem, and Newport also grew into important entrepôts and industrial centers by 1690.

The formidable, often frightening, forest yielded marketable furs and skins as well as fresh game. Everywhere the great trees, towering obstacles at first, fell under the axes of a small army of woodsmen, who produced pipe staves, barrel headings, house and ship timbers, clap-

11. *New England Quarterly*, X, 573.

boards, boards, and other forest products for sale in the English West Indies and which, in time, exceeded fish as valuable exports. The forest also supplied the bulk of the materials for building ships on the Piscataqua, at Boston, and on Narragansett Bay—the largest and most complex technological undertakings of the century.

By 1690 the Yankees had evolved an economy that not only employed all of the people but also yielded a modest prosperity for the majority and made the merchants moderately rich. New England shipping had become so competitive that jealous London merchants persuaded Parliament to pass a series of acts to regulate the trade and navigation of England and the colonies in the interest of the mother country. Many Englishmen believed that the New England shipping threatened their merchant marine. Whether their fears were justified or not, the Puritans of 1630 and their descendants had worked a virtual economic miracle in the new land and were now savoring its sweetness.

Puritanism never was the monolithic, all-inclusive faith that its critics at the time, and since, have thought it was. Like everything else, it had to be adapted institutionally to New England, and the process proved to be both difficult and painful. No approved method for forming a church or installing a minister had been worked out in England. In Massachusetts a group of unusually competent clergymen headed by John Cotton evolved the "Way of the Congregational Churches." Marriage became a civil ceremony instead of a religious rite. To ensure a much needed measure of co-operation among many separate churches, synods were called from time to time and endorsed by the colonial governments or the commissioners of the United Colonies. By such means, the resourceful leaders of church and state worked in concert to produce solutions suitable for a society that was constantly expanding over a very large territory.

In each newly settled town, a church was gathered promptly, if indeed it had not been organized in advance, with an educated minister and, as soon as it could be raised, a meetinghouse. One unremarked accompaniment of this ecclesiastical fission was the astonishing amount of traveling by ministers to attend funerals, ordinations, and synods, and commencements at Cambridge. The clergy also communicated regularly with each other between journeys, and those of Boston maintained a transatlantic correspondence with their dissenting brethren in England. As a result, in nearly every one of the hundred or more towns of New England could be found at least one university- or college-bred, highly educated resident, one whose professional interests and requirements provided bonds of unity not to be found in the colonies to the southward.

The original accommodation of English Puritanism and the frequent adjustments effected thereafter enabled the Congregational churches and their pastors to meet all of the spiritual needs of a religious people. After the mid-century, the emerging Yankees slowly but inexorably leavened the Utopian faith of the Puritan leaders. Old Joshua Scottow might lament the moderating of "the primitive zeal, piety, and holy heat found in the hearts of our parents," about whom Cotton Mather was preparing a book of New England martyrs, but very few of the people (even of the original immigrants) had ever entertained very serious notions about building a city on a hill or did many of them look upon Utopia as desirable. They did not expect a heaven on earth, but, with Mr. Mather, when they thought of a terrestrial paradise, it closely resembled New England. Most of them agreed literally with the words of the preacher: "Let us hear the conclusion of the whole matter: Fear God, and keep his commandments; for this is the whole duty of man." [12]

Puritanism did not fail or degenerate in seventeenth-century New England as so many critics have insisted; it was, as the Reverend William Hubbard proudly recognized, "an incredible successe," which has never been matched. John Winthrop and the principal "forefathers," despite their inbred practical bent, had been inspired, idealistic, and other-worldly at times; but in New England, on occasion, the common sense, down-to-earth, often stubborn mood of the "silent Democracy" of Yankees opposed a healthy realism to the Utopianism of this "Speaking Aristocracy." [13]

Not the least of the many contributions of the ministers to the life of New England was the part they played in education. In 1642, Harvard College, which they had helped to establish, began to graduate young men who soon took over the town pulpits originally occupied by graduates of Cambridge and Oxford. When the college was not in session, youthful Harvardians taught in the town schools, which had been prescribed by law. Many a community raised a schoolhouse, while others used the master's house or the meetinghouse for that purpose. Often, in the smaller towns, the minister prepared one or more promising lads for admission to Harvard College. The result of all this conscientious effort was that, at the close of the century, though Cotton Mather feared a "Criolian Degeneracy" because of the "Want of Educa-

12. In these beliefs, they agreed with Oliver Cromwell (who also knew his Bible) when he instructed his troops to cross a river and attack the Royalists: "Put your trust in God; keep your powder dry." Joshua Scottow, *Old Mens Tears for Their Own Declensions* [1691], (New London, 1769), 5; Ecclesiastes 12: 13.

13. William Hubbard, *A Generall History of New England from the Discovery to MDCLXX* (Cambridge, 1815), 14.

tion in the Rising Generation," illiteracy was low, even in comparison with the mother country. Governor Joseph Dudley wrote to the Society for the Propagation of the Gospel in 1701: "I am of opinion that there are no children to be found ten years old who do not read well, nor men of twenty that do not write tolerably." [14]

The ministers also gave the essential support to the printing press that was set up in Cambridge in 1638, as well as to the one established at Boston in 1674. Most of the output of the New England presses was religious in nature and written by the ministers: sermons, broadsides, almanacs, and a few books. Narrow in range and intolerant in spirit though Puritanism was, in New England it embraced a complete culture such as the people of no other colony experienced in this century, this was the achievement of a devoted group of ministers who were determined not to permit their societies to lapse into barbarism. Not until 1685, when William Bradford opened his shop at Philadelphia, did any other region have the benefits that came with printing.

The leaders who successfully planned the Bay Colony and transported thousands of Puritans across the ocean between 1629 and 1642 also displayed their talents in the political sphere by transforming the charter of a trading company into the constitution of a commonwealth. In Massachusetts, Connecticut, New Haven, and Plymouth, these men proved themselves wise and capable administrators. In 1643, to ensure their common defense, they created the United Colonies of New England,

---

14. In a discussion about congregational singing of psalms, "Jeffry Chanticleer" stated in 1724 of the people of New England: ". . . there is not (I presume) one in a Thousand among us that have not been taught to read." *New-England Courant*, February 24, 1724. Cotton Mather, *The Way to Prosperity* (Boston, 1690), 33–34; Joseph Dudley, as quoted by Edward Eggleston, in *The Transit of Civilization* (Boston, 1959), 267.

which, despite certain obvious defects and the bigotry of excluding Rhode Island, was the first attempt at intercolonial unity in the new world of the English.

These successful colonial adaptations of English institutions on the highest level were accompanied by a possibly more important adjustment in local government. The New England town meeting was evolved out of the parish vestry and radically adjusted to the conditions by divesting it of its ecclesiastical function but giving it several more weighty ones. Above all, participation in the town's deliberations was open to all adult males, a device that permitted the occasional introduction of new ideas, as well as the airing of grievances. Very quickly the town meeting took its place, with the church, as an institution cherished by all Yankees.

The fateful decision for the Puritan host to depart from England and venture all in the unknown wilderness could only have been made by people convinced that a divine plan was being carried out. Their ministers had told them in many a sermon that this would be the culmination of all history, and they believed that they were making very important history. As William Bradford had pointed out back in 1625, many settlers had felt the sweetness of the country. By the spring of 1636, the public mood of the inhabitants of Massachusetts had shifted significantly "as they began to be perswaded they should be a setled People." New England was becoming home for them, and they were coming to love the land where they could live well and, as the old Puritan phrase had it, be merry in the Lord.[15]

In the new homeland the colonists saw the hand of God everywhere and believed that the more memorable events ought not to be forgotten. The Commissioners of the United Colonies agreed in 1646 that "Whereas our

---

15. *Johnson's Wonder-Working Providence*, 118.

good God hath from the first done great things for his people in these Colonies in sundry respects worthy to be written in our hearts with a deepe and charected [engraved] impression not to be blotted out and forgotten and be transmitted to posterity, that they may know the Lord, and how he hath gloryfyed his grace and mercy in our foundations, they also may trust in him"; therefore they directed that in each colony special providences be collected and recorded.[16]

In the preface to a projected history of English America, John Scott, a notorious adventurer and proven rascal, declared: "In my Youth I was a great lover of Geographie and History in Generall," and about 1648, at the age of 18, determined "to make America the scene of the greatest Actions of my Life." He never completed his manuscript for publication in which he planned to describe (for the first time) the English Empire from Newfoundland to the Spanish Main—about 2800 miles in all, but his more than favorable account of New England betrays an abiding affection for the country.[17]

Upon offering *New England's Memorial* to his readers in 1669, Nathaniel Morton quoted John Higginson and Thomas Thatcher as saying: "It is much desired there might be extant A Compleat History of the United Colonies of New-England, that God may have the praise of his goodness to his People here, and that the present and future Generations may have the benefit thereof." "Sundry of the Elder Planters are yet living," and Morton thought that by a sort of oral history project "Materials for a True and full History" might be assembled. It remained for the Reverend William Hubbard to prepare *A Generall History of New England* sometime before 1679,

16. *Records of the Colony of New Plymouth in New England, 1620–1692*, ed. Nathaniel B. Shurtleff and David Pulsifer (Boston, 1859), IX, 82.

17. John Scott's MS fragment is in the British Museum: Sloane MSS, 3662 (paged from the back), 2, 4, 22, 23.

when the General Court of Massachusetts appointed a committee to read it and report back. Not until October 1682, however, did this body order payment of £50 to the Ipswich minister for his record of God's providence and direct him to transcribe it into a book. Although both Cotton Mather in the *Magnalia* and Thomas Hutchinson in his *History* drew heavily from it, the book was not published until 1815. Posterity would like to know more about the vote of the General Court of Connecticut in 1695 thanking "Mr. Stow for his great paynes in preparing a History of the Annals of New England." [18]

The outstanding literary achievement of Puritan New England, indeed of the entire English colonies, was the widely read and influential *Magnalia Christi Americana* completed by Cotton Mather in 1697 and published at London in 1702. The Boston minister sought to reinvigorate the old Puritan zeal of the founders by writing of their lives, work, and tribulations, and by narrating "the Ecclesiastical History of New England." No other work of that time or since portrays so vividly, so completely, and so intimately the characters and doings of those gentlemen leaders. But what is seldom appreciated is the author's great love for New England and his excessive pride in what had been achieved, with divine assistance of course, in the place of his birth. Affection for the country had pervaded the land, though not often so clearly expressed; it may be said that Cotton Mather spoke for the vast majority "in this our New England." [19]

18. Nathaniel Morton, *New-Englands Memoriall* . . . (Cambridge, 1669), "To the Reader"; *Public Records of the Colony of Connecticut*, ed. J. H. Trumbull and Charles J. Hoadley (Hartford, 1868), IV, 144; *Records of the Governor and Company of Massachusetts Bay*, ed. Nathaniel B. Shurtleff (Boston, 1854), V, 278, 378.

19. Cotton Mather, *Magnalia Christi Americana* (London, 1702), I, Attestation by John Higginson, A-2, C-2.

An early instance of what was to become a habit, of using the names New England and America interchangeably, was Nathaniel Ward's remarking in 1647 that "Divers make it an Article of our American Creed" that "no man ought to forsake his owne countrey, but upon extraordinary cause." Three years later Mistress Anne Bradstreet described herself as the Tenth Muse "residing in America alias Nov: Anglia"; and Edward Johnson clearly meant the region when he referred to "these American parts" in 1648 and "the shores of America" in 1650. About the same time, Joseph Rowlandson, charged with libel in the Essex County Court, held that the Court of Assistants alone could try him "by the Lawes of America." And when Captain John Mason addressed his "Briefe History of the Pequot War" (1650) "To the American Reader," he evidently had a regional audience in mind rather than the "american World," as he put it.[20]

During the severe drought of 1662, Michael Wigglesworth of Malden put into literary form his lament that, because of the prevailing pride and wantonness in his beloved country, an angry God had made it "a waste and howling wilderness."

> Ah dear New-England! dearest land to me;
> Which unto God hast hitherto been dear,
> And mayst be still more dear than formerlie,
> If to his voice thou wilt incline thine ear.

20. [Nathaniel Ward], *The Simple Cobler of Aggawamm in America* (London, 1647, reprinted Ipswich, Mass., 1930), 24; [Anne Bradstreet], *The Tenth Muse lately sprung up in America. By a Gentlewoman in these parts* (London, 1650), preface; [Edward Johnson], *Good News from New England* (London, 1648), 12; *Johnson's Wonder-Working Providence*, 32; John L. Sibley, *Biographical Sketches of the Graduates of Harvard University* (Cambridge, 1873), I, 312; *Major [John] Mason's Brief History of the Pequot War*, ed. Thomas Prince (Boston, 1736), iii.

The poet, a second-generation minister and graduate of Harvard, is thinking of the land and the people as his country; he is a New England patriot.[21]

Samuel Sewall, born in England in 1652, crossed over at the age of nine to Newbury, where he attended school under the Reverend Thomas Parker. In 1671 he graduated from Harvard College. When he was representing the Bay Colony at London in 1689, he told a hospitable English dissenter that he considered himself "a Stranger in this Land." There is not the slightest doubt that he had grown to be a full-fledged Yankee. Eight years later he published a forty-page Millenarian tract in which he argued hard that New England ought to be the seat of the New Jerusalem. Most of this work was dull and unconvincing, even in its own day, but Sewall's glowing tribute to Newbury fuses in a classic manner the Puritans' belief that God had led them to the promised land and that the country had a sweetness of its own:

"As long as Plum Island shall faithfully keep the commanded Post; Notwithstanding all the hectoring Words, and hard Blows of the proud and boisterous Ocean; As long as any Salmon, or Sturgeon shall Swim in the streams of Merrimack; or any Perch or Pickeril, in Crane-Pond; As long as the Sea-Fowl shall know the time of their coming, and not neglect seasonably to visit the Places of their Acquaintance: As long as any Cattel shall be fed with the Grass growing in the Medows, which do humbly bow themselves before Turkie-Hill; As long as any Sheep shall walk upon Old Town Hills, and shall from thence pleasantly look down upon the River Parker, and the fruitfull Marshes lying beneath; As long as any

---

21. Michael Wigglesworth, "God's Controversy with New England," first printed in Massachusetts Historical Society, *Proceedings*, XII, 83–93.

free and harmless Doves shall find a White-Oak or other tree within the Township, to perch, or feed, or build a careless Nest upon; and shall voluntarily present themselves to perform the office of Gleaners after Barley-Harvest; As long as Nature shall not grow Old and dote, but shall constantly remember to give the rows of Indian Corn their Education by Pairs: So long shall Christians be born there; and being first made meet, shall from thence be Translated, to be made partakers of the Inheritance of the Saints in Light. Now, seeing the Inhabitants of Newbury and of New-England, upon the due Observance of their Tenure, may expect that their Rich and Gracious LORD will continue and confirm them in the Possession of these invaluable Privileges." [22]

This eloquent burst of pride, affection, and faith of 1697 reveals not merely a "right New-England Man," but it needs very little added patriotic fervor to turn it into the Spirit of '76.

The English colonists had much in common everywhere in the new settlements, whether north or south: their language, basic governmental forms, common law, religious heritage, customs, and, what is often passed by, an inspiring historical tradition that belonged to them quite as much as it did to those of their nation who stayed at home. Furthermore, all the settlers had known the long-lasting and difficult task of establishing new homes in an unfamiliar environment.

22. Consider also, Sewall's pride in Mary Brown [Godfrey], the first person born in Newbury, and still alive in 1697, a mother and a grandmother: "And so many have been born after her in the Town, that they make two Assemblies, wherein GOD is solemnly worshipped every Sabbath Day." *Phaenomena quaedam Apocalyptica ad Aspectum Novi Orbis configurata* (Boston, 1697), 2, 3, 42, 49, 59; *The Diary of Samuel Sewall, 1674–1723*, ed. M. Halsey Thomas (New York, 1973), I, 59, 226.

During the more than eight decades that elapsed between the settlement of the English at Jamestown in 1607 and the series of revolutions in the colonies in 1688–89, it is improbable that many bands of pioneers newly seating themselves south of the confines of New England took much delight in their natural surroundings, let alone felt at home in what they commonly called a howling wilderness. The founding, settling, and developing of new communities along the Atlantic seaboard and on some of the smaller islands in the Caribbean absorbed all of the time and energies of these immigrants, who consisted mainly of young men.

Although Virginia was the first English colony, the growth of a sound and balanced society was very late in coming. Not until 1650 could the contours of a permanent society be discerned. The inhabitants, John Hammond said, began at this time "to grow not only civil, but great observers of the Sabbath, to stand upon their reputations, and to be ashamed of that notorious manner of life they had formerly lived and wallowed in." Until the last quarter of the seventeenth century, a marked scarcity of women severely restricted the formation of families in Virginia, which, in turn, postponed the maturing of its society. Social life was further limited by the dispersed nature of plantation settlement and the lack of towns. As for the land itself, most observers agreed with Morgan Godwyn who, in 1676, found the country both pleasant and fruitful, though it seemed not to have aroused any emotions of love or deep affection.[23]

Contemporary opinion attributed the late development of a true society to the scattering of the population on

23. John Hammond, *Leah and Rachel* (London, 1656), reprinted in Peter Force, comp., *Tracts and Other Papers* (Washington, 1844), III, no. XIV, 9; Morgan Godwyn, *The Negro's and Indian's Advocate* (London, 1686), 169.

widely separated tobacco plantations and the absence of "Townes and Corporations stored with Trades and Manufactures." Between the burning of Jamestown by Nathaniel Bacon's rebels in 1676 and the establishing of Williamsburg as a city in 1699, the colony had no real center at all. The internal isolation of the inhabitants from each other was paralleled by their collective isolation from England, and also even from the other continental and insular colonies save Maryland.[24]

One of the very few Virginians who traveled to colonies other than neighboring Maryland in the seventeenth century, and then usually on official business, was the first William Byrd. He went to New York and Albany on "a public concern" in the summer of 1685. His wife accompanied him and, at Manhattan, gave birth to a son. Five years later, in a letter to Daniel Horsmanden, his brother-in-law living at Purleigh in Essex, England, he remarked plaintively: "Wee are here att the end of the World, and Europe may bee turned topsy turvy ere wee can hear a Word of itt, but when news comes [by the tobacco fleet once a year] wee have it by whole Sale, very often much more then truth; therefore I beg the favour to hear from you as frequently as may bee." [25]

Some of the leading Virginians candidly faced up to the situation. Henry Hartwell, James Blair, and Edward Chilton, the authors of *The Present State of Virginia, and the College*, conceded in 1697 that "the most general true Character of Virginia is this, That as to all the Natural Advantages of a Country, it is one of the best, but as to the Improved Ones, one of the worst of all the English Plantations." As for the House of Burgesses, "the major

24. British Museum: Egerton MSS, 2395, fols. 354, 366–67.
25. William Byrd to Reverend Daniel Horsmanden of Purleigh, Essex, August 8, 1690, *Virginia Magazine of History and Biography*, XXVI, 392; XXV, 46, 48.

Part of the Members whereof having never seen a Town, nor a well improv'd Country in their Lives, cannot therefore imagine the Benefit of" town life.[26]

In the light of this state of affairs wherein even a love of locality had yet to be born and men knew next to nothing about their neighbors in other provinces, it would be unreasonable to expect to find any signs of intercolonial solidarity before 1690. The fabled society of Tidewater Virginia, which ultimately produced such a galaxy of American statesmen, was almost exclusively an achievement of the eighteenth century. One may fix its earliest date at 1693, when the College of William and Mary was founded at Middle Plantation, which was not chartered as Williamsburg until 1699.

Although less populous than the Old Dominion, Maryland greatly resembled it, especially in its southern parts. There the tobacco planters, though seated somewhat closer together, could seldom see the next neighbor's house. The only town, composed of a few houses and a church, was tiny St. Mary's. "We have not yet found the Way of associating ourselves in Towns and Corporations, by reason of the fewness of Handycraftsmen," the Reverend Hugh Jones pointed out in 1696.[27]

As early as 1663 many Quakers moved northward from Accomac County in Virginia to plant tobacco along the Eastern Shore of Maryland from Wye River to the head of Chesapeake Bay and around on the western shore

26. Henry Hartwell, James Blair, and Edward Chilton, *The Present State of Virginia, and the College*, ed. Hunter D. Farish (Williamsburg, 1940), 3, 5.

27. The new settlements in Carolina were not yet sufficiently advanced in 1690; only in and around Charleston in the southern part did any considerable number of people live who could be said to have constituted a society. Hugh Jones, "An Account of Maryland," *Philosophical Transactions of the Royal Society of London*, III, 602; and "Some Observables in Maryland," *William and Mary Quarterly*, 2d series, XXIII, 483.

as far as Gunpowder River. In May 1672 George Fox and a party of Friends made the difficult journey overland from the head of Wye River to New Castle, where they crossed the Delaware, and proceeded across to Middletown, New Jersey, whence a Friend carried them in his own boat to Gravesend on Long Island. By this memorable trip a line of communication was opened from the Eastern Shore to New York and beyond. Quakers, and shortly Presbyterians, would travel increasingly along this route on religious errands, while English, Swedes, Finns, and Dutch farmers and traders started a commercial traffic that would soon draw those Marylanders living around the head of the Chesapeake Bay into the economic and social orbit of the rising town of Philadelphia.[28]

Although no signs of a sentiment of unity or of intercolonial feeling could be discerned in "these American parts," nevertheless by 1690, much had been accomplished, albeit unconsciously, that laid the foundations so essential for the eventual growth of such a feeling among the colonial people as a whole. Over seven decades, the settlers in New England had succeeded in turning the forest wilderness into a flourishing rural and commercial society with a rapidity hitherto unknown; and in the process they had silently transformed themselves into the new Yankee breed and displayed a touch-

28. See William and Thomas Richardson, Account Book, 1662–1702 (MS, Newport Historical Society) for indications of brisk trading relations by Quakers coming by sea to the Eastern Shore and the spreading of Friends' tobacco plantations around the head of Chesapeake Bay as far as the Gunpowder River; also Carl Bridenbaugh, *Fat Mutton and Liberty of Conscience* (Providence, 1974), 114–16. For early travels through the middle colonies, see the *Journal of George Fox*, ed. John L. Nickalls (Cambridge, England, 1952), 618–19, 627, 630–34; and the journey of Cuthbert Potter from the Rappahannock, chiefly by land, to Boston in 1690, in *Travels in the American Colonies, 1690–1783*, ed. Newton D. Mereness (New York, 1916), 4–11.

ing love of their land. Elsewhere, in Virginia, Maryland, and the sparsely settled middle colonies, town life had not yet developed sufficiently to permit the forming of a sense of community or for their people to enjoy the peculiarly colonial benefits of organized religion.

The revolutions of 1688–89 in New England, New York, and Maryland, though but remotely connected, one with another, did reveal the existence of a rising feeling of resentment by many colonists up and down the Atlantic seaboard over the shabby treatment accorded them by the mother country. The revolutionary conditions did, however, bring some of the principal leaders of one region of the colonies to an awareness of and, in some cases, the opportunity for a few of them to get to know one another. Governor Francis Nicholson of Virginia sent Major Cuthbert Potter northward in the summer of 1690 to take the public pulse in each colony. He discovered that the Yankees of Massachusetts were "generally much dissatisfied." This attitude of uneasiness and resentment waxed and waned over the next eighty-five years, during which it contributed to an irrevocable, germinating spirit of colonial unity.

The lack of any material support from across the sea against the French and Indians during King William's War (1689–97) not only aroused much bitterness over such neglect but inspired the first fumbling attempts at common action for intercolonial defense. In the spring of 1690, spurred on by the urging of the General Court of Massachusetts, Governor Jacob Leisler of New York invited all of the colonies from New England to Virginia to send commissioners to a meeting at Manhattan to provide for the common defense. Although Massachusetts, Plymouth, and Connecticut—in the spirit of the United Colonies of old—sent delegates, Rhode Island could not do so but promised financial aid; and Maryland agreed to contribute one hundred men to the military force of 835 men.[29]

In retrospect we can understand that what this first intercolonial effort revealed more than anything else was the difficulty of achieving unified political action without the essential social and economic preparation. Joint political action has to rest upon an underlying public feeling of agreement and commitment. Eighty-four years after the meeting at New York, the American spirit would be spread sufficiently among the people to make the First Continental Congress a success.

29. Potter, in *Travels in the American Colonies*, ed. Mereness, Governor Simon Bradstreet (Mass.) to Governor Thomas Hinckley (Plymouth), April 11, 1690, Massachusetts Historical Society, *Collections*, 4th series, V, 239.

II
The Expanding Intercolonial Community
1690-1740

Back in 1898 two of the nation's most distinguished historians labeled the years between 1690 and 1740 "the neglected period of American colonial history." Today, seventy-six years later, it is still neglected and consequently but little understood; possibly because the period lacked dramatic incidents, the history of those years has been deemed mundane and uninteresting. A closer inspection, however, reveals that during this virtual half-century there took place in the English continental colonies an unparalleled expansion, as well as a steady progress toward consolidation. In those years the inhabitants transformed scattered wilderness settlements into a fruitful rural society with five urban centers at a rate of change unapproached anywhere in the world.[1]

The dynamism of existence in the English colonies at the beginning of the eighteenth century was unperceived in Europe or even by the men and women who participated in it; they were too preoccupied with making and

1. Charles M. Andrews and Herbert L. Osgood, in American Historical Association, *Annual Report for 1898* (Washington, D.C., 1899), 47–76.

doing to realize what they were achieving. As the late Adolph A. Berle wisely observed about our own century: "Americans build fast, but are slow in social thinking." The same comment can be made of the colonial period. In 1739 a perceptive and itinerant botanist, John Bartram, made a proposal for collaboration that years later would produce the American Philosophical Society, the most influential intercolonial organization before the assembling of the First Continental Congress at Philadelphia in 1774. His contemporaries, including such prominent colonials as the Mathers of Boston, Cadwallader Colden of New York, and James Logan, the erudite bookman of Philadelphia, were still thinking in provincial terms. The colonies had not yet produced a leader of continental stature.[2]

All of the progress toward expansion and consolidation of this era was made by the people. A remarkable increase of population had occurred, and the spread of settlements, coupled with material growth, had generated among the inhabitants a feeling of identity with the country. In 1739 the English colonies had existed for 132 years, and to employ an agricultural metaphor, the field had been cleared, plowed, and seeded; and shortly the crop would emerge from the soil, grow, flower, and be ready for harvesting. In other words, between 1690 and 1739 the groundwork had been laid, and shortly immense and irresistible forces of human energy, drive, and determination would be released.

When the period opened the inhabitants numbered about 225,000; as it drew to a close the figure approached

2. Adolph A. Berle, in *The Reporter*, June 28, 1956, p. 10; Peter Collinson to John Bartram, July 10, 1739, *Memorials of John Bartram and Humphry Marshall*, ed. William Darlington (Philadelphia, 1849), 132; and Brooke Hindle, *The Pursuit of Science in Revolutionary America, 1735–1789* (Chapel Hill, 1956), 64, 66–74, for the founding of the American Philosophical Society (1743).

a million. The white population accounted for the largest proportion of the increase, for it doubled about every two decades. To it were added two streams of non-English immigrants who came year after year until the outbreak of the War for Independence. The Scotch-Irish, or Ulster Scots, began to arrive almost immediately after the Peace of Utrecht in 1713; Protestant by faith, even fiercely so, they were also dissenters from the Church of England. The Germans from the Rhenish Palatinate started to immigrate after 1720. They too were Protestant—German Reformed (Calvinists), Lutherans, and Pietist sects.

The irresistible attraction the English colonies had for the poverty-stricken and oppressed people of Europe is vividly brought home to us by the letter that James Murray, a Scotch-Irish schoolmaster, wrote back to "Reverend Baptist Boyd," his minister in County Tyrone. It was printed there for wide circulation in Ireland, and Benjamin Franklin reprinted it on the front page of his *Pennsylvania Gazette* for November 3, 1737: "Ye ken I had but sma Learning when I left ye, and now wad ye think it, I hea 20 Pund a Year for being a Clark to [New] York Meeting-House, and I keep a Skulle for wee Weans: Ah dear Sir, there is braw Living in this same York for high learned Men: The young Foke in Ereland are aw but a Pack of Couards, for I will tell ye in short, this is a bonny Country, and aw Things grows here that ever I did see grow in Ereland; and wee hea Cows, and Sheep, and Horses plenty here, and Goats, and Deers, and Racoons, and Moles, and Bevers, and Fish, and Fouls of aw Sorts: Trades are aw gud here, a Wabster gets 12 Pence a Yeard, a Labourer gets 4 Shillings and 6 Pence a Day, A Lass gets 4 Shillings and 6 Pence a Week for spinning on the wee Wheel, . . . Ye may get Lan here for 10£ a Hundred Acres for ever, and Ten Years Time tell ye get the Money, before they wull ask ye for it . . ." Small wonder that James Murray wants his father, brother, and Mr. Boyd to come over to New York as soon as possible. If they cannot afford the passage money: "I wull bring ye aw wee my sel . . . fear ne the See, trust in God, and he wull bring ye safe to Shore, . . ."

Landing at Boston, New York, Philadelphia, New Castle, or Charleston, the Scotch-Irish and the Germans helped to meet the demand for sorely needed labor, especially in Pennsylvania and the colonies to the southward. Nearly all of the men and boys of this new immigration, as well as many of the women, crossed the ocean as indentured servants in order to pay for their passages. On their arrival they were usually taken off to work in rural areas, which often were in colonies other than that in which they had landed. As newcomers, localism and provincial boundaries meant very little to them; as Protestants, their dissenting views, organization, and preference for supporting ministers by voluntary contributions rather than by taxes set all of them apart from the Anglicans and supplied common ground for opposition to ecclesiastical establishments in New York, Maryland, and the Carolinas. The Germans were more than ordinarily isolated because of the language barrier. It seems as if every incident and aspect of their migrating experience contributed to an intercolonial outlook.

Black slaves, originally from Africa, had been brought into Virginia, Maryland, and the Carolinas, and to a lesser extent into New York in the previous century, but they did not become a large element in the population before 1710, even in the Chesapeake Society. Together with the white indentured servants, the black slaves made up the great labor force that increased the production of staple crops in the plantation colonies during the first half of the century. Without them the rapid growth

and maturing of the famed tobacco society of the Chesapeake and the highly profitable nascent Carolina-Georgia
rice and indigo economy could never have kept pace with
the prosperity of the agricultural-commercial provinces
to the northward or, perhaps, with the late-developing
mixed-farming communities of their own "Back Country." The blacks left no individual records and they
clearly had no voice in determining their own destinies,
but there can be no denying that their collective labors
sustained the southern colonies or that their presence in
mounting numbers constrained the planters to adopt
common policies and attitudes about race discipline.

Whatever may have been the forces that propelled or
expelled the Europeans to the New World, the promise
of land was the lodestone of America. In the new settlements staked out from 1690 to 1739, whether by native-
born pioneers or immigrants, the main attraction for men
and women was the opportunity to make homes for
themselves. Even the descendants of the Puritans craved
fertile farm land as much as they wanted their own
churches and town meetings. A man who acquired land
of his own was willing and expected to expend untold
hours of hard labor to clear and break it, to plant, cultivate, and harvest his crops, and then to carry them to
market. One must not overlook the fact that in this
period, property—its acquisition, possession, and security—was every bit as precious to the people of
America as it was to those in England.[3]

3. At this point it is appropriate to deal with the words *America* and
Americans. The name "United States of America" first appears in
the Declaration of Independence. The late Samuel Flagg Bemis
pointed out that "the proper name *America* is entirely proper to
describe the nation comprised by the United States, and *American*
to designate a citizen of the U.S.A. South American friends have
sometimes thought this presumptuous, but the fact is that the
word was first used in Europe, particularly in the early diplomatic
correspondence of Spain and France. Before the Revolution they

The Scotch-Irish and Germans, frequently led or managed by native-born eastern men of English extraction, filled in some of the extensive unpopulated tracts. From the Penobscot to the Savannah, the distances between villages along the seacoast and in the adjacent interior had shrunk considerably by 1739, and the isolation of farms, one from another, had been reduced. As settlements spread, there gradually developed a need for interchanges: the farmers wanted market outlets for their agricultural surpluses; the people of the seaboard were looking for opportunities to develop trade with the Back Country.

Both the areas and the rate of agricultural expansion are impossible to measure with any accuracy, but the outlines of this rural growth are clear. Boston—perhaps Salem too—needed to import flour, fish, and some barreled meats, plus lumber, wood products, and pig and bar iron; but New England, as a whole, continued to feed itself in spite of the doubling and redoubling of the population. Furthermore a host of new and specialized craftsmen was producing such things as furniture, wheeled vehicles, and boats that added greatly to the comforts of life among the Yankees.

The most notable extension of settlement into what had once been woodlands occurred in the middle provinces, Pennsylvania and New Jersey in particular. There the new immigrants emulated the native-born farmers in raising barley, oats, and buckwheat, but the principal

spoke of *Anglo-Americans*, to distinguish from Spanish Mexicans, Chileans, Peruvians, etc. Afterwards they logically dropped the word *Anglo*. It was only natural for the people of the United States to adopt this European usage, which is now confirmed." *Diplomatic History of the United States* (New York, 1936), 43n. The present writer concurs in this view, and as will become evident in later pages, will adduce further evidence that the English colonists called themselves Americans and referred to their land as America long before the War for Independence.

crops were wheat and corn. While some of the corn was consumed by the families of the farmers, their servants and slaves, most of it was used to feed livestock (cattle, hogs, and some horses). Ships bound for distant markets invariably carried barrels of pork, beef, and marketable quantities of dairy products, salted butter and cheese. Local millers ground increasing amounts of flour and corn meal to ship out; some of the flour was baked into ship's bread. As agricultural surpluses mounted, merchants sent off more and more cargoes of produce to the Caribbean, to France, and the Wine Islands, and even to England.

Tobacco and slaves formed the economic base of the Chesapeake Society, which included Maryland, Virginia, and the Albemarle region of North Carolina. The centers of economic and social activities of this area were Williamsburg and Annapolis, and there the courts and provincial governments convened annually during "publick times." Leading the movement into the Piedmont were scions of Tidewater families in search of virgin and superior land, and they were often accompanied by indentured servants who, upon obtaining their freedom, acquired land of their own and became farmers. By 1720 the celebrated plantation mansions began to appear along the banks of the James, York, Rappahannock, Potomac, and on the western shore of Maryland. Members of this newly risen planting gentry merged into a bourgeois aristocracy, which was nearing its peak in Virginia, for the wealth exhibited in their ostentatious way of living was illusory. The planters, according to Thomas Jefferson, because of extended credit and unpaid debts had become "a species of property, annexed to certain mercantile houses in London," and the same might be said of the planters in Maryland, who were falling into this bondage for the same reasons. All of these planters had closer contacts with England than with their fellow gentry of the north and the south.[4]

Newness was the badge of the Carolina Society, which was just beginning to take definite form at this time. Cattle raising and trade with the interior Indians were giving way after 1713 to the rice culture; and by 1739 rice was king. In many ways South Carolina had served as a buffer colony against the incursions by the Spanish, French, and Indians until 1732, when Georgia, the last of the thirteen colonies to be founded, assumed this responsibility.

In rural sections, industries sprang up because of the great demand for certain articles by the farmers and also because of the availability of essential raw materials. In southern New York, the part adjacent to New Jersey, and New Jersey itself, Pennsylvania, Maryland, and Virginia, the simultaneous presence in the forests of hardwoods for burning into charcoal, surface limestone for a flux, and iron ore gave rise to an industry capable of producing enough iron to meet domestic needs and leave a small surplus for export. The first forge in Pennsylvania was founded by Thomas Rutter in 1716, and by 1739 a total of twenty-two had been erected. Grist mills, sawmills, fulling mills, and rural craftsmen skilled in working up wood and iron increased in numbers in all regions toward the end of the period but especially in New England and among the German settlers of Pennsylvania.[5]

By virtue of the vast extent and variety of the country, each of the geographical regions of the English colonies, including that of the Caribbean, exhibited distinctive fea-

4. "Additional questions of M. De Meusnier, 1786," *The Complete Jefferson*, ed. Saul K. Padover (New York, 1943), 52.

5. Arthur C. Bining, *Pennsylvania Iron Manufacture in the Eighteenth Century* (Harrisburg, 1938), 10, 41, 43, 50, 96, 170, 187.

tures that contributed to an intercolonial division of labor. In addition there were potentially important, though at first invisible and hitherto unnoticed, commercial links.

The internal market of the United States celebrated by Guy Stevens Callender and other economic historians in the late nineteenth century had its counterpart, albeit a far smaller one, emerging in the last two decades of the period ending in 1739. Flour, hauled from the interior counties of Pennsylvania by wagon to Philadelphia or shipped down the Hudson from Esopus to Manhattan, went out in coasters to feed the people of Boston, Charleston in South Carolina, or Bridgetown in Barbados. In time, Lancaster saddles, beaver traps, and Pennsylvania rifles would be transported in great Conestoga wagons drawn by huge horses by way of "The Great Philadelphia Wagon Road" as far south as the Savannah River. In New York, Richard Wistar's famous Philadelphia brass buttons would find a sale, and the leather breeches made in the Quaker town would earn intercolonial repute and be imitated at Hartford in Connecticut.[6]

Ever since 1607 the slow but relentless process of creating wealth out of a forest wilderness had been going on, and by the end of this period the inhabitants collectively had laid up a small surplus. Prospering merchants in the northern seaports tended to devote most of their profits to extending their own shipping ventures, the purchase or building of more ships, the erection of ironworks, or the acquiring of large tracts of land. In the plantation country, the great tobacco and rice growers laid out much of their surplus capital in aristocratically

6. Evelyn A. Benson, "The Earliest Use of the Term 'Conestoga Wagon'," Lancaster County Historical Society, *Papers*, LVII, 109–19.

approved conspicuous display and luxurious living, but their true wealth consisted of broad acres of cleared land and slaves. An impressive portent of the America to be was the widespread and always increasing well-being of the owners of small farms in the middle and New England colonies. Illustrative of the rise of a successful class of tradesmen and artisans in the towns and villages of the northern regions was James Gray who "used to go up and down the Country Selling of Books"; he died at Boston in 1705 leaving "a Considerable Estate," including £700 in coin.[7]

Perhaps no achievement of the Americans has so attracted the attention of foreign observers as the rise in the standard of living among ordinary people. During this half-century it appears to have spurted ahead, and a much larger proportion of the inhabitants shared in it than in any other country of the age. Great fortunes did not accumulate, but neither did poverty keep anybody down who wanted to work, and plantation slaves enjoyed a better and more profuse diet than many a European peasant. Not a few of the colonials, particularly in the towns, could now afford, for the first time, some of the amenities of life. Elementary schooling had become available in many places; the rate of illiteracy of the native-born white population was low; and in New England nearly every child learned to read and write either at school or as a requirement of the system of apprenticeship. A young printer, Benjamin Franklin, headed a group of craftsmen in founding The Library Company of Philadelphia in July 1731, and north of Maryland the idea of subscription libraries spread rapidly.

Any newly settled agricultural society needs, above everything else, commercial connections with the outside

7. *Boston News-Letter*, April 16, 1705.

world and conveniently located centers where goods and produce of all sorts can be assembled, processed, and distributed. Nothing so saliently indicates the dynamic expansion of the English provinces as the mushroom-like growth of the five principal colonial ports of Boston, Newport, New York, Philadelphia, and Charleston, and the signs of emerging secondary communities, such as Portsmouth, Salem, New London, Hartford, and Albany, which would flourish in the thirty-five years before 1775. These urban centers provided not only warehouses, wharves, and docks, but contained in addition shipyards, rope-walks, cooperages, slaughter houses, a variety of metalworking establishments, and some mills. In them, too, the farmer coming into town to market his products found retail shops of many kinds to supply his wants.

The assertion is frequently heard that colonial America—and later the United States—suffered politically, socially, and perhaps most of all, culturally, because it had no single dominant metropolitan center. When the abundant evidence about the many essential services supplied to the hinterland by each of the great towns is weighed, the argument appears shallow and its proponents betrayed by their own ignorance. In the days of sail and the horse, for a vast land with more than 1200 miles of seacoast, neither a London nor a Paris would have met its needs. Once again, there had to be a geographical division of urban services; for the English colonies, the five seaports, now on the verge of becoming small cities, provided a much superior solution to the metropolitan problem. They served not just as commercial entrepôts but as political, religious, and cultural centers, each for an extensive and spreading rural interior. By 1739 Boston had commenced to lose its lead, and Philadelphia, geographically better situated both for coastal and inland intercourse, was moving rapidly ahead in population and wealth.

The settling of large areas of the Back Country from Pennsylvania southward, in New York, and in northern New England dictated a number of improvements in the means of communication; these in turn ensured more frequent exchanges between town and country whereby urban services reached more and more interior communities. The lengthening and widening of Indian paths and packhorse trails, as well as the building of sturdier bridges and safe and better-attended ferries, were undertaken to accommodate the growing cart and wagon traffic connecting the coast with the new inland settlements. So necessary was better transport to the traders and farmers of Pennsylvania to carry the barrels of meats, grain, flour, and other products over the hilly roads to Philadelphia that ingenious rural craftsmen modified and improved a canvas-covered English army wagon for this traffic. Sometime after 1717, James Logan purchased one of these vehicles to haul away the furs assembled at his post on the Conestoga Creek in the present Lancaster County. The Palatines bred the sturdy Conestoga horses, six of which (with bells) were needed to draw a heavily laden wagon. For easier and faster travel along the improved highroads of New England and Pennsylvania, carriage makers at Boston and Philadelphia began to build suitable equipages.

Better highways, bridges, and ferries permitted marked improvements in the colonial postal service, which was established in 1692, and gradually the principal seaboard communities were linked together. By 1698 a route between Portsmouth in New Hampshire and New Castle on the lower Delaware River was traversed weekly by the postriders. When Alexander Spotswood became postmaster general for North America in

1730, he proceeded to reorganize and extend the service; before his death ten years later, the mail routes had been extended as far south as Williamsburg, and the Charlestonians were clamoring for the completion of the coastal route to their city. The appointment of Benjamin Franklin in 1737 as deputy postmaster was an act destined to bolster intercolonial unity.[8]

Uncertain and slow as the first postal service was, its role in drawing the colonies ever closer together has never been fully appreciated. It was the postmaster of Boston, John Campbell, who established the first newspaper in 1704, the *Boston News-Letter*. In an early issue he advertised to sell at the post office six different London newspapers, "either in setts by the year or single." And when Andrew Bradford, the postmaster at Philadelphia started to issue the *American Weekly Mercury* in 1719, he announced that his colleagues at Newport and Williamsburg would accept subscriptions to this second news sheet, whose very title implied the Pennsylvanian's interest in intercolonial communication. Under Spotswood's direction, the postriders were authorized to carry newspapers, as well as the mail.[9]

Twelve newspapers were established between 1704 and 1736 in seven different colonies; only New Hampshire, Connecticut, New Jersey, North Carolina, and Georgia lacked one, but each of these provinces was reasonably well served by the printers of Boston, Philadelphia, and Charleston. Nine journals were being published regularly in 1739. The proliferation of newspapers in these years and the circulation of each one in several colonies and the Caribbean Islands indicate the thirst for general information and business news among the people of all ranks.

8. *South-Carolina Gazette*, December 1, 1737.
9. *Boston News-Letter*, July 30, 1705; *American Weekly Mercury*, December 22, 1719.

In every large town the post office was the center for all intelligence, domestic and foreign, and wherever and whenever the riders delivered a newspaper some obliging person usually read the contents aloud for all present to hear. Up to 1730, at least, these little four-page gazettes turned out to be powerful economic and cultural vehicles contending with the churches as agencies of intercolonial unity, for it is by the number of auditors, not of readers, that their influence must be gauged. The post offices were also the points of departure and arrival for messengers and carriers. There too the traveler could obtain all of the available information about transporting goods and passenger accommodations, either by water or overland, within a given region; stage coaches running between Boston and Newport set out from these offices.[10]

Two enterprising Boston booksellers brought out in April 1732 *The Vade Mecum for America: Or, a Companion for Traders and Travelers,* sure testimony to their belief that a considerable market existed for a guidebook, especially one compiled by the popular and learned Reverend Thomas Prince. Of primary importance in its six sections were "The names of the Towns and Counties in the Several Provinces . . . together with the Time of the Setting of their Courts"; "The General Meetings of the Baptists and Quakers"; and "A Description of the Principal Roads from the Mouth of the Kennebeck River . . . to James River in Virginia," including the distances from Boston and the names of the public houses along the way.[11]

10. *Boston News-Letter,* October 15, 1716; April 4, 1720; May 15, 1721; *Boston Gazette,* August 5, 1728; April 25, 1737; *American Weekly Mercury,* February 25, 1728/9; February 7, 1737/8; *South-Carolina Gazette,* September 23, December 1, 1737.

11. *The Vade Mecum for America* also contained interest and computation tables, the names of the streets of Boston, and geographical information. Improvements along the post road from Boston to New York may be traced by comparing Thornton, Morden, and Lea, *A New Map of New England, New York, New Jersey, Pensilvania, and Maryland, and Virginia* (London, 1685); *The Journal of*

Few aspects of provincial life impress and astonish the investigator more than the sheer numbers of men and women colonists who took to the roads or made coastal journeys by water at this time. To accommodate travelers on the highroads, more inns and taverns opened in the chief towns and villages and at ferry crossings; at the postriders' stages, ordinaries were to be found. Services in these hostelries ranged from very good to very bad, but at any one of them the wayfarer was bound to find an intermingling of all kinds of people, travelers from the north or the south, the seacoast or the Back Country, with whom he might converse and learn the news.

In addition to the unending migrations of the Scotch-Irish and Germans, there coursed along the north-south roads many journeymen looking for jobs in their crafts, schoolteachers, or soldiers on their way home from the wars. Some people were traveling on business; others for religious purposes; people changing residences; and not a few were pleasure bent, to visit friends or to see the country. Even a new criminal element, consisting chiefly of counterfeiters and small bands of horse-thieves, now frequented the highways.

Most of these travelers were cognizant of news in the gazettes, which also gave currency to their activities. The person who won the greatest intercolonial reputation of the century and a half before independence was "the notorious Tom Bell," a Harvard man gone wrong—the first American bunco artist and confidence man. Two years as an undergraduate at Cambridge and a speaking knowledge of Latin had a true practical value, for they enabled him to pass as a gentleman. He owed his amazing success wholly to the possession of information about events and the gentry in colonies other than the one where he was

Madam Knight, ed. George P. Winship (New York, 1935), which contains a map of 1702; and *The Vade Mecum for America*.

impersonating the son of some prominent individual. This "great American traveller" kept himself abreast of colonial affairs by means of the newspapers, but at the same time, these informative sheets spread the news of his rogueries throughout the continent and in the British West Indies, and ultimately brought about the end of his career.[12]

For the benefit of his health, Dr. Alexander Hamilton made a tour on horseback of 1624 miles in length from Annapolis to Portsmouth and back in 1744 accompanied only by his slave Dromo. During his leisurely trip, he encountered Americans of nearly every type and class and found much in life along the way to amuse and divert him. On the final page of his "Itinerarium," he sums up his experience: "I found but little difference in the manners and character of the people in the different provinces as I passed thro', but as to constitutions and complexions, air and government, I found some variety. . . . As to politeness and humanity, they are much alike except in the great towns where the inhabitants are more civilized, especially at Boston." [13]

Many journeys made overland for any distance depended in some measure on water transportation too. From the earliest times, the favorite route of gentlemen traveling from Boston to New York was to go by horseback or in the stage to Bristol Ferry, cross to Rhode

---

12. For Tom Bell's career as an impersonator, schoolteacher, mariner, horse-thief, and inciter of the first anti-Semitic mob in the British dominions to 1740, see *Virginia Gazette*, July 21, 1738; November 16, 1739; *Pennsylvania Gazette*, May 31, June 14, 1739; April 10, 1740; *Boston Evening Post*, September 10, 1739. Up to 1752 nearly every colonial newspaper carried reports of Bell and warnings about his "felonies." The Purdie and Dixon *Virginia Gazette* for July 4, 1771, contained an account of Thomas Bell's execution for piracy on April 25; he died "very penitent."

13. *Gentleman's Progress: The Itinerarium of Dr. Alexander Hamilton, 1744*, ed. Carl Bridenbaugh (Chapel Hill, 1948), 199.

Island, and proceed to Newport, which offered good inns and taverns. From there, with some regularity, vessels sailed down Long Island Sound to Manhattan, where there also were good accommodations. Contrary tides and heavy winds might prolong the voyage by one or more days, but leisurely travelers preferred this to the route of the postriders through Providence, Westerly, New London, Saybrook, and along the stony shore road of Connecticut.

The principal use made of coasters, however, was to collect and distribute European goods and local produce, and deliver parcels and heavier freight. This traffic was heaviest between Boston and Philadelphia, and between Charleston and the sea-island plantations of Carolina and Georgia, as well as to Cape Fear. No detailed study of this coastwise commerce has ever been made, but it is likely that in tonnage, the commerce must have equaled the West Indian traffic and possibly the overseas shipping; and certainly the number of vessels employed would have been greater. True or not, this trade provided a reliable and constantly growing interchange among the five leading colonial seaports, which in turn were linked with the smaller secondary towns and the farms of their hinterlands, and its value and significance cannot be questioned.

Despite many losses during the wars, transatlantic and coastal shipping flourished. The rapid increase and wide distribution of wealth among the common people had encouraged the colonial merchants, especially those from Philadelphia northward, to import larger amounts of luxury goods per capita at the end than at the beginning of this half-century. The newspapers regularly carried the notices of merchants who had received a large variety of "European Goods fit for the Season," and a good market for them arose in remote areas where country storekeepers and itinerant traders dispensed them to their customers. One result of this boom in trade was a growing merchant marine and the employment of more and more sailors.

The rising consumption of imports generated a demand, which other needs of expanding trade buttressed, for some kind of a medium of exchange to replace the gold, silver, and bills of exchange remitted to London in payment for European goods. The issuing of bills of credit, as paper money was then known, was the only substitute. When a currency was carefully managed, as in Pennsylvania, it served the purpose well; but where too many bills of credit were issued and little effort made to retire them periodically, as in Massachusetts, depreciation, inflation, counterfeiting, and other problems inevitably ensued.

The merchants in each of the five metropolitan centers had relied chiefly on the medieval device of conducting their affairs through reliable members of their families located in several key ports. Outstanding examples of this practice were the Huguenot Faneuils of Boston and New York, and the Quaker Redwoods of Bristol, Antigua, Philadelphia, and Newport. All around the periphery of the Atlantic, Quaker merchants, making use of the Friends' meetings to further their material welfare, traded with each other; and similarly, the Jewish traders of Newport dealt principally with those of their own faith at New York, Philadelphia, Kingston, and Bridgetown.

Some members of the mercantile communities gained valuable experience and knowledge of trading in early manhood by acting as supercargoes on colonial vessels bound for the West Indies, the Iberian Peninsula, some port in France, or for Britain; while other lads commenced their careers before the mast and rose, often at a very young age, to be masters of ships. It was not un-usual for some of these young men to set up as agents in faraway seaports before they returned home to settle down as shippers and distributors. As a rule, within a few years, they were presiding over countinghouses lo-cated in their own warehouses, whose contents were brought in by their own ships.

All of this activity enhanced the feeling of solidarity among the members of the mercantile society in coastal and distant ports. Enjoying connections with traders in smaller communities, in the West Indies, and often in England and on the continent of Europe, they began to co-operate, or consolidate, to further common commer-cial and shipping interests. One way, common in pre-vious centuries, was by intermarriage among members of mercantile families. The prime facts for the purposes of this book are the intercolonial role the merchants played, their ever-broadening contacts, and the frequency of their correspondence up and down the Atlantic seaboard.

Commercial friendships were extended and sustained by correspondence, wherein information about prices was exchanged along with political news and personal items. Sent through the colonial post or, more often, en-trusted to the masters of vessels, the shipping papers and correspondence of merchants that have survived from this period provide conclusive evidence of the gradual strengthening of ties among the leading trading com-munities after 1730.

Merchants in one seaport often shared with their fel-lows in another, whom they had come to know and trust, the ownership of vessels, venture cargoes, or special voyages. Perhaps more advantageous to them, particu-larly during wartimes, was the spreading of marine in-surance risks. Almost as important, however, were their many services for each other when acting as agents or at-

torneys in matters involving contracts, the quality of provisions, fair measures, payment of crews' wages, and a
host of other legal affairs. In truth, the legal aspects of
shipping and commerce prompted the passage, largely at
the solicitation of the merchants, of a considerable body
of legislation, which would eventually be reflected in the
"full faith and credit" clause of the Federal Constitution.

Urban merchants rarely restricted their interest to
maritime affairs, for nearly every one of them sold goods
from a shop in his house or warehouse, by wholesale or
retail, to townspeople and countrymen; they outfitted
hawkers and peddlers and supplied goods and credit to
the keepers of general stores in the interior villages. At
Charleston, Philadelphia, and Boston some of the more
successful merchants had, in addition to working capital,
sums of money that they advertised to lend out, thereby
performing the role of bankers as had the Medici in
Florence and the Fuggers of Augsburg.

The success of the local, provincial, intercolonial, and
imperial pursuits of these men, as well as the safety of
their investments in ships, credit, cargoes, insurance, and
sometimes industrial ventures, rested largely upon their
reputations for honesty (they never enjoyed the anonym-
ity provided by the modern corporation). The great majority of them evinced high degrees of individual probity
and responsibility, as well as shrewdness, and their reward was that, by colonial standards, they grew rich.

As merchants and planters accumulated wealth, approved standards of taste, prestige, and display impelled
them to build fine town houses or impressive mansions
on rural estates, to fill them with beautiful furniture and
plate, and to use them as backgrounds for elegant wining
and dining, often too for dancing and gambling. These
were the quintessence of social diversion. When their
ships were out at sea and they were without obligations

to any community, the town merchants had more leisure
to become well informed through conversation and debate in clubs, and also time to read and devote to cultural
interests. In fact, these men of the countinghouse and the
planter-merchants had gone a long way toward forming
the first social class, one that extended far beyond the
boundaries of any single province by 1739. During the
three decades that followed they would prove themselves
to be a capable and responsible bourgeois aristocracy
sprung from American soil.

The pre-industrial economy of the English colonies
grew very rapidly after 1690 and, after 1720, seemed to
surge forward. For twenty of the fifty years of the
period, warfare of some kind was going on, a condition
that accelerated at the same time that it retarded colonial
development; in the final analysis the wars undoubtedly
stimulated this remarkable growth. In all newly settled
areas the same familiar processes went on: trees and underbrush had to be cleared away, stubborn virgin soil
first broken up, then crops planted, fields fenced, and
frame buildings put up. Such a vast expenditure of
human toil might appear at first glance to have been
merely preparatory, but the fact that slowly and la-
boriously a substantial amount of new wealth was being
created cannot be ignored. Much of this wealth belonged
to ordinary folk whose counterparts in Britain or Europe
would have possessed little if any landed property. Moreover, the new wealth was transferable: improved lands
could be bought and sold.

Supplying flour, corn meal, butter, and salted meats to
the English and colonial troops, and ship's bread and
similar foods for the constantly enlarging merchant
marine, privateer crews, or naval personnel provided the
first American opportunity to profit from war contracts.
Piracy in the 1690's, then privateering, followed by clan-

destine trade with the enemy or forbidden traffic with the Spanish, Dutch, and French colonies after 1713, brought in sorely needed supplies of coin. So it was in the early eighteenth century that pieces of eight, or dollars, first began to appear almighty to the Americans.

The common hazards of conflict forced at least a few colonists into an awareness of the pressing need for cooperation of many kinds, though between 1690 and 1740 very little progress was actually made in concerting efforts. One cannot doubt, however, that wars did speed up improvements in communications among the colonies and increased both trade and travel within them.

On the other hand the wars had demoralizing results. For the first time, outbreaks of crime and food riots occurred in Boston where the costs of the abortive expedition to Quebec had led to a depression; and poor refugees, driven from northern New England by French-inspired Indian raids, became burdens on the poor rates of Boston and other coastal towns. To add to these woes, the enemy captured or sank many valuable ships and cargoes. Everywhere, including Charleston, political stresses and high public costs created unrest and strained colonial loyalties to the mother country at a time when thousands of immigrants who had never felt any loyalty to Britain or affection for its rulers were swarming into the country.

Most of the difficulties stemmed either from friction aroused by the presence of the English military and naval forces or indignation that these same forces did not afford them better protection. In 1707 English naval officers contemptuously accused Andrew Belcher and other Boston traders of profiteering in supplying food for the forces; they also complained about the lack of discipline, the stubbornness, and the ill-will among the colonial troops. The Yankees countered with sharp indictments of military indifference and inefficiency and, most of all of the galling and scarcely concealed English attitude of superiority about everything colonial. The dismal failure of the Walker Expedition against Quebec in 1711 brought forth a flood of charges and countercharges from both sides. In New York and northern New England the settlers insisted bitterly that they had received no help from Britain in their struggles against the Indians (who were attacking from French Canada). John Adams recalled in later years that as a lad of ten in 1745, his head was full of tales about Church, Lovewell, and the famous Indian fighters: "I heard a number of old men who had been a soldiering . . . at the Eastward, relate their dangers, escapes, combats, and enterprises," and from such sources gained "a very high opinion . . . of my countrymen . . . In the same years I heard great complaints of the English, of their neglect to defend us and assist us." [14]

Far to the south, without any support from the outside, the Carolinians had to contend with the Spanish in Florida and the Indians at home. In 1711–12, Colonel John Barnwell went out from Charleston to the northern part of the huge province and defeated the Tuscaroras; Governor James Moore finally crushed them the next year; in 1715 the uprising of the Yamassees had to be put down at great expense of lives and treasure by the Charlestonians. Encirclement by the Spanish in Florida and the French, who were growing stronger at their new settlements of Mobile and New Orleans, was also a source of great worry to them. Fair and even-handed distribution of the blame between provincial selfishness and English neglect or assessment of the merits of colonial pride as opposed to imperial arrogance is impossible at

14. John Adams to Mercy Warren, July 20, 1807, Massachusetts Historical Society, *Collections*, 5th series, IV, 338–39.

this date, but the resentments aroused in this period were perpetuated and never forgotten.

Traces of the sentiment for keeping America out of the quarrels of Europe can be found in the earliest years of the Puritan settlements in Massachusetts. Two outstanding illustrations, which resulted from warlike attitudes on the far side of the Atlantic in the eighteenth century, clearly reveal the prevalence of an official Yankee mood. Tiring of conflict, which benefited neither party, Governor Joseph Dudley of Massachusetts proposed to Cavagnal Pierre Rigaud de Vaudreuil, governor of Canada, a treaty of neutrality in 1705. Agreement was never reached because the French insisted upon including New York and the other English colonies in the plan and the exclusion of New Englanders from fishing in Acadian waters and the Gulf of St. Lawrence. That the initiative had come from Massachusetts was significant, however.[15]

The action of the House of Representatives of Massachusetts taken on December 30, 1734, when there seemed to be some likelihood of war between "the Crowns of Great Britain and France," was intended to forestall any resulting calamities from falling upon Massachusetts and the neighboring provinces; this was the second important instance of the drift of colonial opinion. The House desired Governor Jonathan Belcher to concert with other governors in the event of a rupture in Europe: "That His Majesty's Subjects in these Dominions may live in a state of Neutrality with the Subjects of the French King . . . on this Continent, as to the affairs of the War, more especially that the Barbarities of the Indians may be prevented for the future." The Council concurred and the colony's agent in London was in-

15. Francis Parkman, *A Half Century of Conflict* (Boston, 1897), I, 103.

structed to pursue the matter with the proper authorities. That nothing ever came of such a proposal is scarcely surprising, but the boldness of a leading colonial assembly in attempting to influence imperial foreign policy could only have strengthened the suspicions held by officials at Whitehall that unless the colonies were strictly regulated they might seek to become independent. Whether the colonists actually had any ideas of such a move is problematical, but at any rate Massachusetts and her neighbors in New England were in no state of mind to accept with equanimity the treatment that would soon be accorded them during the hostilities of the War of Jenkins' Ear and King George's War.[16]

The great emphasis customarily placed upon particularistic features of colonial politics, such as perennial disputes over boundaries, currency troubles, and the reluctance of individual assemblies to appropriate funds for military use or to send troops to serve in other colonies, while important matters, ought not to obscure other aspects of colonial history.

Many legislative actions of the eighteenth century reflected the experience of the settlers fifty or a hundred years earlier. The very planting of a colony in Virginia in 1607, where none before had existed, and of every succeeding settlement with the exception of Massachusetts were in some respects unconscious acts of independence. In the latter instance of 1629, the going out of Britain was a planned enterprise and a deliberate rejection of much that was English. From 1634, when Archbishop Laud's Commission called for the vacating of their charter, the leaders of Massachusetts, always supported by the rank and file, openly defied the royal authority; and in the time of the Civil War and the Interregnum

16. *Journals of the House of Representatives of Massachusetts, 1715–1776* (Boston, 1931, 1932), XII, 165; XIII, 67.

(1641–60) they conducted the affairs of their colony as though it were an independent republic. Charges made in 1660 and succeeding years that the management of a trading company by minting coins, denying appeals to England, and executing Quakers among other acts had assumed attributes of sovereignty were certainly not wide of the mark. In sharp contrast to the "isolationist policy" of Massachusetts was the widespread loyalty to King Charles I in Virginia under Governor Sir William Berkeley.

Upon the restoration of the Stuarts, London merchants, court officials, and Parliament moved jointly for the first time to frame a colonial policy that would foster English shipping and trade and draw the overseas dominions closer, politically, to the mother country. The Puritans, slow to recognize King Charles II, went along grudgingly, but local officers did very little to enforce the acts of trade, allowed their merchant acquaintances to traffic openly outside of the commercial system, and obstructed investigation of their activities by a royal commission. In one instance the General Court actually held that an act of Parliament did not apply to Massachusetts Bay unless it was passed again by the Court.

English patience finally ran out, and in 1684 the charter was vacated; New Hampshire was detached from Boston's overlordship, and all of New England was consolidated under a royal governor. Deprived of the virtually complete self-government enjoyed for more than a half-century, even of their treasured town meetings, all land titles placed in jeopardy, and left to face the Franco-Indian threat on their frontiers alone, the ordinary people of New England, as their resentment rose, could find very little in the English connection to cherish or even to respect. The outcome of the Revolution of 1688 was the resumption of what they had long considered to be their liberties: security of property and persons, the Congregational form of worship, and self-government.

After the suppression of Bacon's Rebellion in 1677 that paved the way for greater control from Whitehall, a royal commission did almost nothing to correct the abuses in Virginia that had produced the uprising. In Maryland and New York similar revolts occurred in 1688–89. Separately and in different ways, the leaders in each colony sought to emphasize that Englishmen in America ought to enjoy the same liberties, privileges, and immunities as those remaining at home, but in every case the royal officials gave them to understand that they were colonials and that no co-equal status could be admitted. Plymouth ceased to be a colony in 1691 and Massachusetts became a quasi-royal province with a royal governor; the crown's authority over Virginia, Maryland, New York, and Pennsylvania noticeably tightened. These experiences, common to all, cut deeply into the pride of the provincial upper class, and inevitably the largely unvoiced feelings of men of property and influence in every province were bound thereafter to focus more and more on grievances and less and less upon demonstrations of loyalty and regard for the monarchy.

This current of questioning the relationships with the mother country was only beginning to flow; it would speed up and slow down at different times in different places. Among the few men who concerned themselves with such matters, however, republican rather than monarchical ideas soon would seem to be more appropriate guides to action in their restless societies. Conspicuously calling himself "An American" on the title page of *An Essay upon the Government of the English Plantations on the Continent of America*, published at London in 1701, an unidentified Virginian expressed the as yet hesitant and ambivalent, confused view of most of the provincial gentry, but he also spoke constructively for them when he wrote: "That by a Free Constitution of Government, I mean, that the Inhabitants of Plantations may enjoy their Liberties and Estates, and have Justice equally and impartially administered to them; and that it should not be in the Power of any [royal] Governour to prevent this." [17]

In the fifty years after the colonial phase of the Glorious Revolution, many things, besides the troubles with the Indians and stresses of war, exacerbated rather than soothed colonial sensibilities. The rise of the press and the founding of newspapers provided ways for religious, political, social, and economic news and opinions to reach ever-widening audiences and to form a rudimentary public opinion. Printed sermons and pamphlets were performing the same office and creating an uneasiness in the minds of men.

English authorities had allowed every colony a representative assembly, and the persisting encroachment of these bodies on the royal prerogative in contest after contest—first with proprietorial, then with royal governors—was the outstanding political development of the eighteenth-century history of the king's dominions prior to 1763. Little by little the lower houses won the right to initiate legislation and control appropriations, and by 1739 this process was well advanced and self-government was a fact. In every province members of the assemblies carefully imitated the procedures and assumed the privileges of members of the House of Commons, while their constituents increasingly looked upon their assemblies as

17. "It is a great Unhappiness, that no one can tell what is Law, and what is not in the Plantations," this anonymous "American" complained: "But the last and greatest Unhappiness the Plantations labour under, is, that the King and Court are altogether Strangers to the true State of Affairs in America, for that is the true Cause why their Grievances have not been long since redress'd." *An Essay*, 17, 46.

being, each within its territorial limits, a miniature parliament; an uneasy truce was reached by several colonial legislatures with "foreign" governors (either royal or proprietary). In the meantime, all but a handful of the men at Whitehall and Westminster remained ignorant of what was going on across the sea. Candidly, one must concede at once that the colonial assemblies usually acted for local and provincial interests and seldom for any intercolonial good, but beyond all doubt their steady encroachment on the prerogatives of royal governors was portentous, and before long would become ominous.[18]

The tradition of dissent, which in many respects had made the colonies founded before 1690 a series of religious experiments, continued to mold provincial life in the eighteenth century when it was both broadened in content and given a fateful new direction. The coming every year of thousands of Scotch-Irish made the Presbyterians the strongest denomination outside of New England by 1739. The immigrants from the Palatinate, as mentioned earlier, divided into three groups: the German Reformed, who were strict Calvinists, the Lutherans, and the Pietists. So widespread, well-organized, and influential by 1732 had the Society of Friends become that the Reverend Thomas Prince included the dates of the set meetings of the Quakers and also those of the Baptists in *The Vade Mecum for America.*

A century or more of exciting religious adventures at home and in the colonies had taught the ministers and leading laymen of the several Protestant denominations to be acutely aware of the affinity between religious and

18. According to Lord Percival's diary, in 1730/1, Lord Baltimore said prophetically: ". . . the islands and plantations on the [North American] continent are in a miserable condition, and in a few years will sett up for themselves purely from the hardships put upon them." Earl of Egmont MSS, *Historical Manuscripts Commission*, I, 151.

political liberties. The latest advices concerning ecclesiastical matters both at home and abroad were, to them, a vital matter. Besides corresponding frequently with their co-religionists throughout the colonies and meeting with them for ecclesiastical business, they opened and maintained lines of communication with their brethren in London, Scotland, and Holland. Far better organized than political leaders, these groups of ministers were in a position to learn about proposed official policy and specific measures that might affect their liberties before the clergy of the Church of England in America could find out about them.

Although the subject demands prolonged investigation, it can be confidently stated at this point that the view of Britain and things English held by the colonists, even by the Anglicans in the southern provinces, down to the year of revolt was always one seen through dissenters' spectacles. Moreover this was as true of their political and social outlook as it was of the religious, and the importance of this fact cannot be overstressed. The superbly effective systems of transatlantic communications, together with their intercolonial counterparts, maintained by the Friends, the Congregationalists, the Presbyterians, and Baptists, were running smoothly decades before certain political leaders shrewdly adopted some of their agencies for purposes of their own. One has but to turn the pages of the newspapers of this period to realize how much the printers were beholden to the ministers for news.

At the turn of the century the hierarchy of the Church of England, urged on by Henry Compton, Bishop of London, took belated steps to recover lost ground on the continent of North America. Its powerful missionary movement, commendable as it was, cannot be disassociated from the contemporary actions of English officials to tighten political control over the colonies. Furthermore, the founding of The Society for the Propagation of the Gospel in Foreign Parts (1701) and its first efforts to send a bishop to America took place in the midst of the Anglo-French wars when other kinds of resentments and suspicions of the mother country were running high. Congregationalists all over New England and Presbyterians in the middle colonies were stunned and outraged in 1722 by the apostacy at New Haven when the Reverend Timothy Cutler, the rector, and several tutors of Yale College repudiated the validity of Presbyterian ordination and decided to cross the ocean and take orders in the Church of England. Interpreted as a threat to cherished liberties, one that would not stop at provincial boundaries, the incident aroused intercolonial repercussions.

While the pressures of external competition were spurring transatlantic and intercolonial action among the leaders, a restlessness was developing among the common people in all of the churches except the Anglican and the meetings of the Society of Friends. This perturbation inspired a series of revivals among the Dutch Reformed worshippers in the Raritan Valley of New Jersey by the Reverend Theodore Freylinghuysen late in the 1720's. Influenced by him, John and William Tennent began to lead revivals among the Presbyterians in the same region in 1733, while independently, Jonathan Edwards of Northampton, Massachusetts, reported surprising conversions in 1735. But it took an evangelist from overseas to demonstrate that these local manifestations of the spirit were symptoms of a religious malaise existing everywhere in the English settlements; the people were only awaiting a leader. In November 1739 the evangelist George Whitefield landed at Lewes, Delaware, and proceeded at once to Philadelphia, which he knew to be the principal religious center. Here he began to preach daily, and thousands of people stood "in an awful Silence to hear him." [19]

The Great Awakening had commenced. No writer has summed up this revival more succinctly and perceptively than Herbert Levi Osgood. "It was the first great and spontaneous movement in the history of the American people, deeper and more pervading than the wars and yet far less prolonged, an event, which in its origin and continuance lay outside of the sphere of influence of governors, councils, and boards of trade." Elsewhere he calls it "an event of general human significance," and it may be pointed out that this amazing emotional outburst could never have unified the colonists had it not been for the half-century of remarkable growth and integration that preceded it. [20]

The rapidity with which the Great Awakening spread over the land, leaving not a single individual wholly unaffected, demonstrates that the inhabitants of the thirteen colonies in 1739 were becoming aware that they were a people, if not yet a nation. The many English among them had behind them a long tradition and a history of nearly a century and a quarter in this good land and they had made it their own. The years since 1690 had been full of trials; but collectively the inhabitants had proved that if confronted with difficult problems they could solve them. Neglected by the mother country, they had held off the French and Indians. The land was theirs, and the idea that nearly every white colonist might possess some of it was theirs alone, not English, not Eu-

---

19. *Pennsylvania Gazette*, November 8, 15, 1739; *Boston Gazette*, December 3, 1739.
20. Herbert L. Osgood, *The American Colonies in the Eighteenth Century* (New York, 1924), III, 409–10.

ropean. Of these and like matters men rarely spoke, but they felt them deeply. Provincials to a man, they were modest about their accomplishments. Whether they were Quakers in Virginia or Yankees at Plymouth, they were using the same words to describe their land—"these American parts"—and they were doing so with pride and a surging self-confidence in the future of the provinces. For the wisest of them, this self-confidence was more than parochial.[21]

21. The Quarterly Meeting of the Society of Friends, Isle of Wight County, Va., to the London Yearly Meeting, March 11, 1696/7, *William and Mary Quarterly*, 2d series, VI, 89.

III
Mounting Self-Confidence
and Gradual Alienation
1740-1760

The deep sense of a continental community—economic, social, and cultural, though not yet political—attained during the two decades 1740–60—was not only unprecedented and unanticipated but, for the most part, uncomprehended by the great body of the colonists of those years. When they spoke or wrote publicly, they did so as provincial members of a great overseas empire and referred to themselves as Englishmen; but in their hearts and occasionally when talking with like-minded friends, many of them were beginning to entertain doubts and becoming conscious of feelings discordant with their old views. By 1760 a society that was recognizably American was bursting into flower. Between the 133rd and 153rd years of a signally rapid recapitulation on the continent of North America of the history of the human race, the inhabitants of the thirteen English colonies experienced an acceleration of the process of growth and integration that, almost overnight, fused them into a fascinating new kind of society.

Aided and sustained by better means of travel and transportation, communications improved, not merely between individuals but also among various newly formed agencies and organizations. The inevitable result of this augmented volume of interchange was an attachment or sense of unity that gained wider acceptance each year and became the principal force in creating public opinion. There was an acknowledged love of "our country" and a growing affection for its people that went beyond the love of the land and one's own locality so deeply felt by Samuel Sewall in the previous century. Although the emotions of most colonists remained unarticulated, not a few men were beginning to use with pride the magic words *America* and *Americans*.

A special feature of the exhilarating effect of the new, broadened patriotism was a conviction about the strength of the colonies as a whole. A century and a half of success in transforming a wilderness into a prosperous countryside served by busy towns, which anyone could see round about him, could breed only optimism. As with any new society, mellowness did not accompany material achievement, and an understandable self-confidence was frequently overblown into an uncritical belief in the ability of the colonists to perform deeds and carry out ventures far exceeding their capacities. Sometimes, too, a dissonant self-assertiveness and braggadocio could be heard in the land, which, however, were but the normal attributes of lusty, inexperienced youth.

At the very time that the colonials were discovering their collective achievements and becoming conscious of their nascent power, there occurred a series of confrontations between themselves and the English authority that gave rise to resentments and frustrations. As one overt act followed close upon another, many of the colonists began to distrust both the good will and the competence of the English, and by the end of the period, more than one of them expressed disgust with the British connection. On many occasions, too, they had cause to question whether the rulers in the mother country sufficiently appreciated the contributions and sacrifices made by the colonies for the good of the empire and, in view of them, were willing to weigh colonial opinion in their decisions. We have seen that as far back as 1689 a few provincials entertained such suspicions, but from 1740 onward, the callous indifference on the part of the British etched these suppositions ever deeper in the minds of more and more colonials. England and her leaders were about to reap the whirlwind.

The year 1739 marked the setting in motion of two powerful forces that irreversibly changed the direction of American history. The first was the resumption of open warfare after a quarter of a century of peace: war with Spain, and in 1744, war with France. During these same years, fierce border conflicts with Indian tribes went on in the southern, as well as the northern, colonies. The Treaty of Aix-la-Chapelle (1748) brought about a truce, but it only lasted four years; the French and Indian War, which began with the fall of Pickawillany on the Miami in the summer of 1752 and ended on the American continent in 1760, finally removed the Gallic menace from the colonial frontiers. Three years later England and France concluded the Treaty of Paris. Throughout these two decades, there were only four years without openly conducted hostilities on land and sea; war was the normal condition, and its effects on colonial society were profound.

The religious movement, the second powerful force to begin in 1739, spread through every colony, as Herbert Osgood pointed out; to view it as an almost exclusively New England phenomenon, significant principally for the history of ideas, is to miss its central importance. It may properly be labeled a revolution, for it fundamentally altered and permanently shifted the direction of colonial life. Above all else, the events of the Great Awakening gave the mass of the people an awareness of American unity for the first time.

There was nothing actually peaceful, tranquil, boring, or normal about existence in the English colonies during these twenty years of foreign wars and religious upheaval. Nor were the material developments of the time at all commonplace, as a few prescient Europeans slowly realized. Born in Naples in 1728, three years after Dean George Berkeley wrote the famous line "Westward the course of empire takes its way," Abbé Ferdinando Gagliani, sometime before 1756, had glimpsed the future of America. Writing in the year of Independence, he advised Mme. d'Épinay concerning her proposed change of residence in Paris: "The epoch has come of the total fall of Europe, and of transmigration to America. Everything here turns into rottenness—religion, laws, arts, sciences—and everything hastens to renew itself in America. This is not a jest; . . . I have said it, announced it, preached it for more than twenty years, and I have constantly seen my prophecies come to pass. Therefore, do not buy your house in the Chaussée d'Antin; you must buy it in Philadelphia." [1]

The Neapolitan priest and other perceptive European *philosophes* derived their enlightened, and often romantic, ideas of English colonial life chiefly from books of travel and correspondence, and only occasionally from publications issued by the printers of Philadelphia and Boston. The most impressive of the latter genre was *Observations Concerning the Increase of Mankind, Peopling of Countries, etc.*, written in Philadelphia by Benjamin

1. Abbé Gagliani to Mme. d'Épinay, from Naples, May 18, 1776, in *Abbé Ferdinand Galiani Correspondence avec Mme. d'Épinay . . .*, ed. Lucien Perey and Gaston Maugras (Paris, 1889), II, 443.

Franklin in 1751 but published in Boston and London in 1755 and frequently thereafter. In it the printer set forth the view widely held by provincial thinkers that the colonial population, because of early marriages, a high birth rate, and easily acquired land, doubled itself every twenty-five years, a growth not even approached in the Old World.

Between 1740 and 1760, the number of inhabitants in the continental colonies rose from slightly less than a million to one-and-a-half million—immigration slackened noticeably in these years—but Ezra Stiles, basing his calculation on the belief that population doubled every two decades, predicted in 1760 that by 1860 the Congregationalists of New England would have increased from 440,000 to seven millions, while the number of Anglicans in the same period, starting with 12,600 would be only 185,000. This contemporary, unshakable optimism about the bright future of "our country" being mathematically demonstrable by right reason was therefore judged scientifically valid.[2]

Fully aware of the fact that the expansion of settlement by the immigrant Scotch-Irish and Germans, as well as by many native-born settlers of English extraction, was filling up the interior lands, the alert colonial *philosophe* Ezra Stiles, pondering the occupation of the new territory to the westward recently won from France, uttered a profession of faith in the *manifest destiny* of the Americans a full eighty-five years before the famous maxim ever got into print. For an agricultural people, his formulation of the promise of America was unmatched: "Free and absolute tenure of *land* and unburdened property, as well as *liberty in religion*, are necessary to tempt us." The

2. *The Papers of Benjamin Franklin*, ed. Leonard Labaree (New Haven, 1961), IV, 225–34; Ezra Stiles, *Discourse on the Christian Union* (Boston, 1761), 114.

prevalence of such conditions in northern New England and from Pennsylvania southward did tempt settlers by the thousands into the greatest movement of people in the century.[3]

The population of the principal seaboard cities continued to mount during these decades, and a dozen or more secondary communities appeared on the colonial scene. The story is a familiar one and needs no repeating, but for present purposes, it needs to be stressed that every urban center, by its very nature and activities, fostered colonial unity. In all of them a notable mixing of people went on daily. Philadelphia with more than twenty thousand inhabitants had replaced Boston as the leading metropolis, and the spectacle of its residents "enjoying every comfort and elegance and even luxury that the first town in Europe could offer" only seventy years after its site had been "a Wilderness" struck one visitor from the Old World in 1755 as a "singular Anecdote in the History of Man." The central location of the city, the improving network of highways connecting it with other seaports and the interior, and the swelling immigrant traffic west and south along the Great Philadelphia Wagon Road made it a Mecca for many purposes other than trade—among them hospital and medical treatment, schooling, and libraries. It was there in May 1744 that Benjamin Franklin, following out the suggestion that John Bartram had made to Peter Collinson of London in 1739, issued a broadside proposing the establishing of a society to promote useful knowledge "among the British Plantations in America." The printer explained: "The first Drudgery of Settling new Colonies, which confines

3. Stiles, *The Christian Union*, 114–15, 121*n*.

the Attention of People to mere Necessaries, is now pretty well over; and there are many in every Province in Circumstances that set them at Ease, and afford Leisure to cultivate the finer Arts, and improve the common Stock of Knowledge." [4]

Franklin hoped to unite in "one Society of Virtuosi" by means of correspondence, the ingenious men "residing in the several Colonies." Although John Bartram, Cadwallader Colden of New York, and several other gentlemen in New Jersey and Virginia joined in the scheme, the war with France diverted attention, and in about a year's time, the society was moribund. This initial venture in forming an American Philosophical Society, premature as it turned out, did launch the idea of uniting talented men, an idea that never died. A second attempt in the 1760's proved a great and permanent success. [5]

The bustling city of Philadelphia not only ranked first in economic importance after 1739, but it overtook Boston as the religious capital of the colonies. In the city, as well as on the continent, the Presbyterians were coming to be the largest denomination; and it was more than ever the center of Presbyterianism following the union of the synods of New York and Philadelphia in 1758. Also, to the city on the Delaware, the members of the Society of Friends, the rising body of Baptists, and the Germans of the Reformed and Lutheran communions looked for leadership; and at least once a year they flocked into town to attend meetings, synods, or conventions, to listen eagerly to famous preachers, to purchase devotional works, or to

4. Thomas Pownall, *A Topographical Description of . . . America . . . ,* ed. Lois K. Mulkearn (Pittsburgh, 1949), 130; *Papers of Benjamin Franklin,* ed. Labaree, II, 378–83.
5. *The America of 1750: Peter Kalm's Travels in North America,* ed. Adolph A. Benson (New York, 1966), I, 31.

arrange for publication of sermons and tracts. No longer did the appellation the Quaker City adequately describe this community.

The infectious influence of the Great Awakening and its long aftermath penetrated nearly every recess of colonial existence. There is no denying the importance of the theological cleavage between those colonists who largely eschewed reason and those who rejected "enthusiasms" and all the emotional features of the revival; but as "the first great and spontaneous movement in the history of the American people," the Great Awakening both embraced and transcended its more narrow theological and institutional features. It was the instrument that promoted the Americanizing of religion in all the colonies, which is our immediate concern.

The unifying and Americanizing of religion is best observed in the cities and towns. It was in Philadelphia that George Whitefield commenced his great work, and he soon carried it on in New York, Boston, Newport, and Charleston, and in the smaller towns as well; men observed at the time that "he chiefly confines his Labours to populous towns"; this was not a frontier business. Only large towns could accommodate the throngs of people who flocked to hear the Word.

Having learned of the thousands of men and women who had heard Whitefield preach at Philadelphia, New York, on Long Island, in Boston, and Hartford, and of the astonishing numbers of conversions to Christ, Nathan Cole, a curious Arminian living in Connecticut, wanted nothing so much as to hear this famous evangelist. Early one morning while he was working in his fields, a friend rode up and told him that Whitefield was to preach that same day, October 3, 1740, at ten o'clock. Dropping everything, Cole rushed to his house, told his wife to be ready to leave immediately, then went out to saddle the horse. With his wife mounted behind him, he started for Middletown, twelve miles away. When the horse tired, Cole would dismount, put his wife in the saddle, run along side until he was exhausted, and then remount. As they approached their destination, they perceived a great cloud in the distance that turned out to be dust raised by more than four thousand people, coming from miles around, on foot or on horseback, to listen to Mr. Whitefield's message. Cole came away converted: "And my hearing him preach, gave me a heart wound; by Gods blessing: my old [Arminian] Foundation was broken up, and I saw that my righteousness would not save me." It was necessary to be reborn.[6]

The astonishing concourse of auditors represented every class and condition of colonists: the gentleman and the indentured servant, the black slave from Africa, the Palatine who understood not a word of English; some were rich and others were poor, there were soul-starved or merely curious persons; they came from the city, the towns, the farms, or backwoods clearings. These gatherings, totally without any European precedent, even dwarfed those of the First Crusade in the number and enthusiasm of the participants. Men and women traveled miles, many of them crossing provincial boundaries, all of them rushing to hear Mr. Whitefield pointedly dismiss all sectarian differences as inconsequential. Such a commingling of believers and scoffers (most of whom were moved if not won over by the call for a New Birth) could not but generate a sense of brotherhood among all colonials without regard to province or sect.

Ordinary people now had something to talk about as they journeyed to and fro and at their work. At nearly

6. *Boston Evening Post*, November 10, 1740; for the moving and revealing account by Nathan Cole, see *William and Mary Quarterly*, 3d series, VII, 590–91; *Boston News-Letter*, June 26, 1740.

every place where Dr. Alexander Hamilton stopped on his leisurely ride from Annapolis to Portsmouth and back in 1744, the "discourse turned chiefly upon religion." This was particularly the case at evening sessions in roadside taverns. The emotional state of the proponents of "enthusiasm" and the mass of their followers was very high, and at revival gatherings they discovered that others too were in a holy heat. Though conservatives deplored the repudiation of reason by the New Lights and New Siders, some of them had to concede the disappearance of many of the old resentments against ecclesiastical authority and that there was greater hope for all men in the substitution of the doctrine of the New Birth than in the old one of election. Similarly, the strengthening of congregations, even in New England, in contests over ministerial or synodical authority imparted a democratic quality to church government.[7]

It is well known that the religious revolution had unifying, as well as divisive, consequences, but that the nationalizing tendency eventually triumphed over the disruptive ones is seldom mentioned. Colonial Protestantism had risen out of a totally different historical experience from that of the European. It was an adaptation to the situation in the new land, and the religious upheaval ensured that certain conditions present from the earliest days would become permanent features of an American religion.

The celebrated English conservative, Edmund Burke, perceived this intuitively and expressed it in 1775 more succinctly and felicitously than most colonials ever did: "Religion, always a principle of energy, in this new people is in no way worn out or impaired; and their mode of

---

7. *Gentleman's Progress: The Itinerarium of Dr. Alexander Hamilton, 1744,* ed. Carl Bridenbaugh (Chapel Hill, 1948), 111, 117, 161, index s. v. religion.

professing it is also one main cause of this free spirit. The people are Protestants; and of that kind which is the most adverse to all implicit submission of mind and opinion. This is a persuasion not only favourable to liberty, but built upon it. I do not think, Sir, that the reason of this averseness in the dissenting churches from all that looks like absolute government, is so much to be sought in their religious tenets, as in their history." [8]

One aftermath of the religious revolution, which was at first disruptive, came in time to draw certain elements in the several colonies together. This was the drive for education. As a defensive gesture in reply to the charges by the Presbytery of Philadelphia that many of its ministers were poorly educated, the Presbytery of New York procured a charter for the College of New Jersey, which opened in 1747 at Elizabeth Town. Significantly, this institution offered "equal Liberties and Privileges . . . to every Denomination of Christians." Meanwhile excellent academies conducted by New-Side ministers opened in southeastern Pennsylvania to compete against the academy founded at New London in 1743 by the Old-Side pope, Francis Alison. Samuel Blair established one at Fagg's Manor, Samuel Finley started another in Nottingham, and Robert Smith conducted a good school at Pequea, Pennsylvania. In the history of liberty in America, the failure of the Presbyterians to procure the founding of a non-sectarian college in New York looms large; the opening of King's College (Columbia) under Episcopal auspices (somewhat limited to be sure) brought about a torrid controversy that raged over an actual institution. [9]

With the founding in 1764 of Rhode Island College

8. "Speech on Conciliation with America," March 2, 1775, in *Edmund Burke Selections*, ed. Leslie N. Broughton (New York, 1925), 149.
9. *New-York Gazette*, February 2, 1747.

(later Brown), in part to train Baptist ministers, the opening of Dartmouth College in New Hampshire in 1770, and of Queen's College (Rutgers) by the Dutch Reformed at New Brunswick a year later, the evangelical impulse to promote higher education ceased. Students traveled from all over the colonies to attend colleges; the College of New Jersey, eventually located at Princeton, filled the pulpits of churches through the southern provinces with its graduates. Higher education, by enabling many future leaders to become acquainted in the classroom and to study a common curriculum, was definitely a unifying force.

The rise of the dissenting sects and the resulting spirit of opposition to any religious establishment, whether that of the Church of England or the Congregational churches in Massachusetts and Connecticut, came about with the religious upheaval. First the Quakers, then the Baptists, Presbyterians, and Moravians struggled at different times against constituted ecclesiastical authority with varying degrees of success; but always the dissenting group talked and argued in terms of liberty of conscience.

The possibility that the missionaries backed by the Society for the Propagation of the Gospel in Foreign Parts might win support at home for establishing the Church of England in the middle and northern colonies prompted the most conspicuous resistance to ecclesiastical authority in this period. Though the Society enjoyed little success, its maneuverings to win adherents by taking advantage of the splitting of congregations into Old Lights and New Lights aroused great fears and suspicions; resentments of Anglican intrusions alerted the Congregational leaders and stiffened their opposition. During the years 1747–50, Edmund Gibson, Bishop of London, made several determined attempts to have a bishop sent over to America to strengthen the Episcopalian foray into New England, where good and sufficient churches had existed for more than a century. In the resulting confrontations, the excellent communications the Yankee parsons had established with their counterparts in England, the Dissenting Deputies, paid off, for Sir Robert Walpole, responding to pressure applied by the Deputies, rejected the schemes.

The New England clergy were quick to mount a counterattack against the "fixed Prelacy" of episcopalianism in their colonies. The Reverend Noah Hobart of Fairfield opened the controversy in an ordination sermon in 1746 and two years later, in a tract displaying a deep historical knowledge and noteworthy skill in debate, he shrewdly referred to the Anglican missionaries as belonging to "the Episcopalian Separation." In 1750, one of the great pulpit orators of the age, Jonathan Mayhew of the West Church in Boston, clarified and simplified the issues of religious liberty in *A Discourse Concerning Unlimited Submission, and Non-Resistance:* "People have no security against being unmercifully priest-ridden but by keeping all imperious Bishops, and other Clergymen who love to lord it over God's heritage, from getting their foot into the stirrup at all . . . In plain English, there seems to have been an impious bargain struck up betwixt the scepter and the surplice for enslaving both the bodies and souls of men." Here, in language adroitly calculated to arouse a people fresh from struggles over clerical authority in their local churches, this able propagandist summarized Mr. Hobart's arguments, which many listeners and readers had already been closely following in sermons, pamphlets, and the newspapers.[10]

The great religious issue in the province of New York

10. Jonathan Mayhew, *A Discourse Concerning Unlimited Submission and Non-Resistance* (Boston, 1750), [vi–vii], 23, 52.

was the denial of equality before the law to the Presbyterians, Lutherans, and Dutch Reformed majority of the population by the Episcopalian royal governor and council in the name of the establishment of the Church of England in that province. Dissenting bodies could not legally own property, such as church edifices or graveyards, and the refusal of the small Anglican minority to open King's College freely to all denominations perpetuated bitter feelings.

Ever since the first settling of New England, and to a somewhat lesser degree elsewhere, the manifold and diverse questions of religion had always weighed more heavily than any other issue in the public expressions and unvoiced sentiments of the colonists. This truth was evident everywhere in everyday speech, and of course in Sabbath discourses. The prevalence of widespread literacy and a well-established press, in addition to the universality of the Great Awakening, served to fuse many religious matters and to foster a rapid growth of public opinion. This was an urban phenomenon.

The colonial newspapers matured and increased in numbers in these years. Counting those journals already in existence in 1740 and those started in the years following up to 1760, twenty-seven newspapers were published between Boston and Charleston; sixteen were still being issued regularly in the last year of the period. The small size of the circulation of a paper bore little relation to its importance, for as mentioned earlier, the true index of its influence was not how many read it but how many people learned the news from it. Furthermore the newspaper audience of readers and listeners widened continually. Dr. Hamilton always put up at the best hostelry for strangers when he reached a town. At Portsmouth on the Piscataqua, he returned to his lodgings at about eight o'clock after paying a call, and "the post being arrived, I found a numerous company att [the Widow] Slater's reading the news. Their chit chat and noise kept me awake 3 hours after I went to bed." [11]

The inhabitants in town and country bought the newspapers to read the latest news on the wars, religious polemics, shipping notices, and advertisements. Although in the aggregate, religious subjects dominated the news in the forties, secular topics began to appear somewhat regularly. There were essays on medical and scientific matters appearing in their pages before they came out in pamphlet form. The religious excitement led to the printing of many sermons, and the presses also poured out tracts and pamphlets on religion, and even books. Ezra Stiles's *Discourse on the Christian Union* became a bestseller in Boston; Edes and Gill told the author they made more on it than on any previous sermon.

The newspaper, understandably, took its place as the most potent vehicle for bringing about unity in public opinion. The clipping of news items from the gazettes of one region for reprinting in the columns of one in another place, and the printing of letters and advices—one suspects them to be deliberate plants at times—ensured a weekly exchange of unmeasurable importance. In this way the printers in the great towns did more to make the widely separated colonists conscious of common religious, social, and economic interests than any other group, even including the ministers. The sense of community that they helped so much to inculcate was the great and necessary preparation for the momentous political developments of the next fifteen years.

Improvements in methods of communication, especially with the interior, by means of new and better roads, ferries, bridges, vehicles, and ordinaries for trav-

11. The physician was having breakfast at Gibb's tavern in Milford, Connecticut, on August 29, 1744 "and while I was there the post arrived, so that there came great crowds of the politicians of the town to read the news, and we had plenty of orthographical blunders." *Gentleman's Progress,* 120, 125, 127, 166.

elers, went forward every year. Stage lines across the Jerseys connected Philadelphia and New York making possible a faster and more comfortable journey. Between the five cities and some of the larger towns, coastal packet boats, sailing more frequently and regularly, facilitated communication along the routes by carrying passengers and letters, as well as parcels and freight; and under the superintendence of Benjamin Franklin the overland post was extended and speeded up. Manhattan became the western terminus after 1750 of the monthly transatlantic packet service.

Striking testimony to the greater desire of the colonists to know more about the land in which they lived, aroused in part by the wars, was the market for a number of maps of the colonies. The first of this notable series appeared in 1749: *A Map of Pennsylvania, New Jersey, New York, and the three Delaware Counties*, by "the ingenious Engineer" Lewis Evans, published at Philadelphia. Joshua Fry's and Peter Jefferson's *A Map of the Inhabited Part of Virginia, containing the whole Province of Maryland, with Part of Pensilvania, New Jersey, and North Carolina* came out in London in 1751, and four years later John Mitchell's *A Map of the British Colonies in North America*, probably the most important "historically and politically" in all American history. In 1755 also appeared Lewis Evans' *A General Map of the Middle British Colonies*, engraved by James Turner of Philadelphia and published there, a map in some respects superior to Mitchell's. These maps, advertised in the colonial newspapers and sold by booksellers in the principal towns, found a ready market. Besides being beautiful representations suitable for hanging on walls, they enabled many a colonist, for the first time, to visualize the country he loved, the relation geographically of one place to another, and their distances apart. And on the Fry and Jefferson revision of 1755, many men must have traced with

wonder and enlightenment the course of "The Great
Wagon Road from the Yadkin River through Virginia to
Philadelphia, distant 435 Miles." [12]

It was in these years of the religious revolution, and
later, that men with intercolonial reputations made themselves heard. Nearly all of them were ministers: George
Whitefield, most famous of them all, was known up and
down the entire coast, but there were Gilbert Tennent
and several other great New-Side Presbyterians, Ezra
Stiles and Jonathan Mayhew, Old-Light Congregationalists, and Samuel Johnson, Anglican leader and first
president of King's College.

Possibly more significant—at least more prophetic—
was the emergence as public men of non-political persons
whose reputations spread beyond the provinces in which
they lived. Among these laymen was William Livingston, the "Independent Reflector" of Manhattan, who
stood out as a doughty controversialist and publicist;
Lewis Evans of Philadelphia lectured in his own city,
Newark, Charleston, and the West Indies on mechanics
and natural philosophy, drew two excellent diagrams for
Franklin's account of Pennsylvania fireplaces, and prepared the several revisions of his map of the middle colonies, which was paid the compliment of being twice pi-
rated. And of course there was Benjamin Franklin,
printer, who enjoyed, perhaps, the widest reputation as
an intercolonial figure; a visible proof that there could be
such an individual as an American *philosophe*. *

That the colonial genius for forming voluntary associa-

12. William P. Cumming, *The Southeast in Early Maps* (Princeton,
    1958), plates 57, 58, 59; Lawrence S. Gipson, *Lewis Evans* (Phila-
    delphia, 1939), maps II–VI at end of volume. See also *Plan of the
    British Dominions of New England in North America . . . by Dr.
    William Douglass* (London, 1753).

* In contrast the only important political figures were William Pepperell of Portsmouth, the conqueror of Louisbourg, and Thomas
  Hutchinson of Massachusetts, both of them relatively obscure in
  1760.

tions to further good ends (displayed long since) could be directed toward colonial unity became evident in two instances. In November 1740 a fire devastated Charleston; it consumed "the most valuable Part of the Town" and wiped out the assets of the Friendly Society, which had been formed in 1735 to insure houses against loss by fire. Letters and accounts of the disaster printed in the Massachusetts and Pennsylvania newspapers inspired humane responses from distant quarters: Boston churches took up large collections to aid the distant sufferers, and the Philadelphia Quakers subscribed £300 for the relief of their fellow Christians. In the northern colonies, George Whitefield raised substantial sums for an orphanage at Ebenezer, Georgia, and for a charity school at Philadelphia. Sympathy and Christian benevolence for the unfortunate poor, orphaned children, or the needy and distressed members of a national group were displayed by the organization, on an intercolonial basis, of friendly societies by the Scots, Irish, Huguenot, and Welsh residents in the leading cities. Dr. Hamilton carried letters of introduction to every prominent and wealthy compatriot living between Maryland and New Hampshire, which eased his progress among the Scots of America. He attended a meeting of the Scots Charitable Society in Boston in 1744 and placed a generous contribution in the poor box. The increase in charity everywhere reflected mounting wealth, but nowhere more than at Charleston.[13]

During the seventeenth century, the Puritan ministers had rehearsed over and over in the pulpit what they called "the errand into the wilderness." It was their answer to "Why did we come into this land?" To some extent the Quakers, the Presbyterians, the Baptists, the

13. *Boston News-Letter*, January 15, 22, 29, May 7, 1741; *South-Carolina Gazette*, May 14, 1741; *Gentleman's Progress*, 133, 242.

two largest German sects, and even in some measure the "plain people" asked this question. It was to exercise the rights of conscience and private judgment according to their lights that they had come over the ocean. It was to enjoy religious liberty.

The ferment begun by the Great Awakening had obviously altered the definition of these liberties. With profound insight, Edmund Burke was referring to this era in 1775 when he warned the House of Commons: "All Protestantism, even the most cold and passive, is a sort of dissent. But the religion most prevalent in our northern colonies [including the Presbyterian, Baptist, and Quaker] is a refinement on the principle of resistance; it is the dissidence of dissent, and the Protestantism of the Protestant religion. This religion, under a variety of denominations agreeing in nothing but in the communion of the spirit of liberty, is predominant. . . ." [14]

The religious revolution had split the colonial churches, and in the middle and New England provinces the efforts of the Anglicans to profit by the divisions had bred genuine fears about the security of the religious liberties of the people. Since 1689, with remarkable learning and logic, Congregational ministers had been demonstrating that the law of God and the law of Nature were one, because a threat to one was a threat to the other; and historians among the clergy had worked out, in several widely read—and reread—works, a native version of the explanation of the errand into the wilderness. For years the pulpit and the press had been reiterating these ideas. However, the toleration, forced by the Great Awakening, and other allied consequences of the movement had generated a powerful thirst for complete religious freedom.

14. *Edmund Burke Selections*, ed. Broughton, 149–50.

A long series of ominous threats by the Crown, the Parliament, and the hierarchy of the Church of England to establish the Anglican church in all of the northern colonies had been successfully resisted by 1760 when Ezra Stiles called for union by all dissenting groups to protect "the precious jewel of religious liberty" against "a formal attempt" that he saw being launched. "Let the grand errand into *America* never be forgotten," he cried. Noah Hobart had already declared that "These American Colonies" were no longer a wilderness. Leadership by resourceful and learned men in the pulpit still held sway at the end of the period, and patriotism was still firmly grounded in religion; but the political tide was coming in strong, and a civil ingredient would shortly be mixed with the economic, social, and religious.[15]

The effects of the last two French wars on colonial society, though not as great as the changes wrought by the religious unrest, were nevertheless far-reaching. Of their stimulus to commerce and agricultural growth, there is no question, but there were psychic traumata coming out of the conflict that augured ill for the Empire. The first time that the king of England ever called upon provincial troops to serve in campaigns not immediately adjacent to their own territories was for the projected capture of Cartagena in 1741, and, later on, Cuba. Their prompt and loyal response must have been heartening. In the very first issue of *The General Magazine, and Historical Chronicle For all the British Plantations in America*, Benjamin Franklin stated that thirty-three companies were being sent to Jamaica from nine colonies for service on the expedition to Cartagena.[16]

15. Noah Hobart, *A Second Address to the Members of the Episcopal Separation in New-England* (Boston, 1751), 31; Stiles, *The Christian Union*, 28, 30, 96, 102, 126.
16. *General Magazine, and Historical Chronicle* (Facsimile Text Society, New York, 1938), January 1741, p. 74; *Boston News-Letter*, March 5, 19, August 13, 1741.

During March and April 1741 came the news of the total failure of Admiral Vernon's effort; the April issue of *The General Magazine* reported from New York that "out of 3500 Men, there is but 1500 Men left, and even all those starving." Other sources gave slightly different figures, but all agreed that fevers, the bloody flux (dysentery), and "Captain Punch," plus insufficient and bad food, had caused high mortality among the colonial troops. In addition, Admiral Vernon had broken up companies of "Troops raised in America" to fill the crews of his ships, pressed men from colonial privateers for the same purpose, and sent others ashore to labor along side of blacks in cutting wood for fuel. An expedition to Cuba was abandoned as a failure in December 1741, and the following March another, directed at Panama, proved a fiasco. In November 1742 British transports carried the remnant back to the continent—only about 10 per cent of the original contingent survived.[17]

For the first time provincial suspicions arose about the military and naval competence of the English. Bitterness, evident at the very start, over a rift between the English and their hitherto loyal colonial supporters was everywhere manifest. As early as March 1741 the admiral had referred derisively to the continental forces as "Americans"; by August the English were being labeled in the northern newspapers in the same vein as "Europeans." These pejorative distinctions also appeared in the dispatches sent back to London. To cap the condescension with which they looked down upon the provincials, English officers frequently branded them as bad soldiers—many as cowards—fit only to cut wood. Tales of such slurs and indignities got a thorough airing in the newspapers when the troops came back, and the mood of disil-

17. *General Magazine*, April 1741, p. 284; Albert Harkness, Jr., "Americanism and Jenkins' Ear," *Mississippi Valley Historical Review*, XXXVII, 61–90.

lusionment became a permanent constituent of public opinion. On January 4, 1742/3, for example, the *Pennsylvania Gazette* carried a report that Benjamin Franklin had clipped from a Boston journal: "It is a very melancholy Reflection, that of the five hundred Men sent from this Province in five Vessels at the first Embarkation, besides Recruits, sent at sundry Times since, (not to mention two or three hundred sent from Rhode Island) there should not be a sufficient Number left to employ one Vessel to bring them home." [18]

Provincial dejection turned to exhilaration close upon the end of the dismal West Indian venture, however, when New England troops led by William Pepperell of Kittery Point in Maine took the great French fortress at Louisbourg on Cape Breton Island in June 1745. From the Piscataqua to the Ashley and the Cooper, the rejoicing was universal, unrestrained, and prolonged. The printers of all newspapers, while commending Admiral Sir Peter Warren and the royal naval forces for transporting the soldiers to Cape Breton, emphasized the magnitude of the New England achievement, which to them was truly intercolonial. Before the fall of the fortress Lewis Timothy enthusiastically told the readers of the *South-Carolina Gazette:* "The French say our Men fight like Devils; for go which Way they will, the[y] are popping at them like true Indian Hunters." At Annapolis "Philo Muses" published a thirteen-verse "Ode in Honour of New England" to preserve the memory of this glorious event:

> Shall brave NEW ENGLAND'S GLORY fly
> Thro' Earth, Air, Sea, and fill the Sky,
> Resounding loud Applause:

18. *Boston News-Letter*, September 17, 1741; July 22, August 26, 1742.

> Shall distant Poets raise the Strain,
> and Neighb'ring Muses on the Main,
> Be silent in the Cause?" [19]

When Governor William Shirley, returning after the capture of Louisbourg, addressed the General Court of Massachusetts, he stated his belief that widespread reporting of the exploit would "reflect a lasting Honour upon the Collonies," for the troops had faced difficulties that none but themselves surmounted. Lewis Timothy reprinted these remarks for the benefit of his Charleston readers, and in August 1746, "Publicola" stated that it was up to the Commons House of Assembly to contribute 1000 barrels of South Carolina rice for the projected invasion of Canada. That much of this outburst of pride and soaring self-confidence in a great common victory was uncritical lessens in no way the proof of emerging Americanism, which it symbolized.[20]

At Boston, where the forces for the expedition to Louisbourg had assembled in the spring of 1745, press-gangs, taking up men and boys from coasters, wood boats, and fishing vessels, "Most arbitrarily and illegally," had infuriated the inhabitants. Many skippers of small craft added to the Bostonians' problems by refusing to make their usual deliveries of wood and provisions lest they be taken up also. Petitions by the selectmen and the town meeting were of no avail; the ships sailed for Cape Breton carrying the impressed seamen.

These incursions were recalled when Commodore Charles Knowles returned from Louisbourg in 1747 and sent out a press-gang to make a general sweep on the

19. *Maryland Gazette*, January 14, October 21, November 25, 1746; *South-Carolina Gazette*, May 10, 1740; June 22, August 9, 1745; *Pennsylvania Gazette*, July 25, August 1, 1745; September 4, 1746.
20. *South-Carolina Gazette*, March 3, August 4, 1746.

night of November 16. Seamen from merchant vessels in the harbor and along the shore were seized, sometimes entire crews; and sailors, longshoremen, craftsmen, apprentices, and laborers were taken up indiscriminately around the wharves. All joy over the victory at Louisbourg was forgotten, a great mob arose, militia men refused to turn out to suppress the tumult, and for several days government was at an end in the worst riot in the colonial history of Boston. The threat of Commodore Knowles to bombard the town if those of his officers held as hostages were not returned alienated and outraged the inhabitants still further. Though the Bostonians could properly claim that theirs was the best regulated community in the British Empire and that government had failed to protect them against the press-gang, Governor Shirley and others blamed the Knowles riot on "the Mobbish turn in this town." The last straw, bringing pessimism and despair, was the news that, under the Treaty of Aix-la-Chapelle, Louisbourg and Cape Breton had been returned to France.[21]

A thoughtful New England man reviewed relations with the mother country in an article in the *Independent Advertiser*, which was reprinted on the front page of the *Pennsylvania Gazette*, December 20, 1748. After enumerating the gains to the "nation" of the conquest of 1745, the writer asks: "but what returns have we received and what advantages has *my Country* derived? Has she gained the favour of the British M———sty by her glorious Achievements?" The answer was a detailed list of grievances against Britain: lack of reimbursement for the cost of the expedition; the giving of prize money to

21. "Records of the Selectmen, 1741 to 1753," pp. 115, 125; "Boston Town Records, 1742 to 1757," pp. 127, 129–30, *Report of the Record Commissioners of the City of Boston* (Boston, 1887, 1885), XVII, XIV; Colonial Society of Massachusetts, *Publications*, III, 214–16.

men who never fired a shot; naval neglect of defense to prevent the recapture of the stronghold; violent and brutal conduct by press-gangs; and the return of Louisbourg without any consideration of what that would mean to New England. "Perhaps this goodly land itself—even *this* our beloved Country, may share the same fate with this its conquest—may be the purchase of a future peace!" Drawing back from overtly arraigning "our lawful and undoubted rulers," this Yankee declares that even slaves may mourn at their pleasure:

"Yes, O my much lov'd country, thee I will lament with the most tender, though unavailing grief!—Nor shall time, which lessens all other mourning, erase from my brest [*sic*], while I live, the memory of thee—*esto perpetua* would be my wish for thee, yet if fate had decreed otherwise, I can only wish thou mayst die in character, and not dishonour the great glory thou hast won; and as thy name will necessarily live to future times, it may be said of thee, *Thou lived gloriously and fell bravely.*" [22]

Provincial resentment over British condescension and discrimination in matters of rank and precedence during the French and Indian War (1754–63) is a familiar story that culminated with the withdrawal of Colonel George Washington from the forces, but what is not so well-known is that the preceding decade was punctuated with incidents calculated to belittle the colonials. References to the rank and file of New Englanders as Yankee Doodles must have reminded old campaigners of the label "Americans" used in the Caribbean; and each time the terms of derision were transmuted into terms of pride.

The succession of disheartening British reverses commencing with Braddock's defeat on the Monongahela in 1755 and continuing almost without let-up until 1759,

22. *Pennsylvania Gazette*, December 20, 1748.

did nothing to revise provincial opinions that reached back to 1739 about the incompetence of English commanders and the superiority of provincial gunfire. Critically and understandably, though in some respects wholly without reason, local faith in provincial prowess and the superiority of the militia over the regulars mounted rapidly as respect for British capacities declined, though of course the same could not be said of the work of the navy. Colonial eyes tended to focus upon the successes of privateers sailing from their own ports and bringing home prizes. James Wolfe's mighty triumph at Quebec and his expressed contempt for the colonial private soldier were too often forgotten as the colonists celebrated the exploits of a Washington and a Rogers. Furthermore, wealth was accumulating in New York and Philadelphia from lucrative army contracts, commerce was flourishing, and population increasing noticeably. Who can condemn them for their optimism?

A considerable body of evidence exists that even among traveled, well-read, and urbane members of the gentry, English and British practices at home and abroad no longer inspired awe. The versatile James Logan of Philadelphia had admitted to Peter Collinson in 1736 that " 'Tis true we in America are little inferiour things in comparison of you great folks in London." But he moved ahead with the country, and in July 1746, did not hesitate to tell John Whiston, the London bookseller, that he who had "been a buyer of Books above these 50 years" was "not to be put off as a common American." [23]

At the impressionable age of twenty-two, John Dickinson crossed from Talbot County, Maryland, to London to spend three years at the Middle Temple and, inciden-

23. James Logan to Peter Collinson, June 8, 1736, Letterbook A; Logan to John Whiston, July 27, 1748, Letterbook, 1748–50, both in Historical Society of Pennsylvania.

tally, to learn much about politics and English society. His first visit to the House of Lords, sitting as a court, produced the following report to his father:

"This noble assembly has not the awfulness I expected. They meet in a room much inferior to that appointed for the representatives of Pennsylvania. The nobility in general are the most ordinary men I ever fac[e]d, and if there is any judging by the heaviness and foppery of their looks and behavior, many of them are more indebted to fortune than their worth for a seat in that august place." The open bribery and corruption in parliamentary elections appalled the youthful lawyer: "It is grown a Vice here to be virtuous." Notwithstanding the diversions, all that could be learned about mankind in England, he wrote his mother, "I shall return to America with rapture. There is something surprizing in it, but nothing is more true than that no place is comparable to our native country." Where a cosmopolitan like Benjamin Franklin found England a perpetual delight and desired to make it his home, most Americans agreed with the estimate of John Dickinson, who would shortly earn the title of the "penman of the Revolution." [24]

From about 1720, with the rise of the newspaper press, an intercolonial public opinion on issues confronting the colonies was clearly discernible, and events between 1740 and 1760 served to broaden and strengthen it. It was without parallel in the Western World or, thus

24. "It is some strange affection nature has implanted in us, for her wise ends," Dickinson continued. "America is to be sure a wilderness, and yet that wilderness to me is more pleasing than this charming garden. . . . But when I think of America, that word produces a thousand pleasing images; it is endeard by my past pleasures there, by my future prospects. . . . I can bear no comparison between it and any other place. Tis rude, but it's innocent. Tis wild, but it's private." See his letter in *Pennsylvania Magazine of History and Biography*, LXXXVI, especially pp. 259–60, 268, 269, 274–75, 421.

far, in modern history; and only a handful of inquisitive Englishmen ever grasped this fact before the War for Independence. Sooner or later the colonists up and down the Atlantic seaboard, stirred emotionally by the religious upheaval and fearing the uncertainties of the nearly continuous conflict, became concerned about the threats they had heard or read about to the land they occupied, owned, and loved. In sermons, pamphlets, but chiefly in the gazettes, the American note was being sounded with more volume and more often.

The titles of two new publications issued at Philadelphia in 1741 clearly reveal this new perspective: *The American Magazine* and *The General Magazine, or Historical Chronicle For the British Plantations in America*. In 1743, Franklin named his proposed organization The American Philosophical Society, and in his persuasive argument for the defense of Pennsylvania, *Plain Truth* (1745), he wrote of "American arms." As each year of this period rolled by the words *America* and *American* and the unifying ideas associated with them were mentioned with greater frequency. Ezra Stiles's reference in his sermon of 1760 to "the grand errand into *America*" expressly implied not just New England, as of old, but all of the continental colonies.

Politics, as everyone knows, thrives on parties and differences over procedures in government; it fosters division more often than agreement, and nearly always promotes contention. This Benjamin Franklin fully understood, and as a man of moderation he deplored the internecine strife engendered by colonial struggles for political power. The mere existence of thirteen separate governments, frequent disputes over boundaries, and the inability of leaders to work out an acceptable plan of union at Albany in 1754, together with similar but minor problems in individual colonies which rose again and again, were all political matters certain to divide men rather than to unite them for some common effort. Thus far we have been examining the economic, social, and religious facts that were consolidating the colonists into one American people; there were, in addition, a few elements of provincial politics that contributed to the same end.

The Independent Whig and other London publications, which emphasized the rights that all Britons ought to enjoy, found a ready sale in the bookshops of Philadelphia, New York, and Boston from 1720 on, particularly after 1740. Possibly the most influential of these was *The English Liberties, or The Free-born Subjects Inheritance*, attributed to Henry Care, a Quaker. A handbook of nearly 300 pages, including many documents and charters, it was first published at London in 1680. James and Benjamin Franklin brought out a fifth edition at Boston in 1721 for Daniel Henchman who, exactly twenty years later, was again advertising the book for sale.[25]

As the Reverend Noah Hobart was preparing his classic case for religious liberty to counter an anticipated extension of the Anglican establishment into New England in 1749, he instinctively included a treatment of civil liberties in his argument; one of them seems to have been introduced by him for the first time on this side of the water. He denied categorically that any law of England for establishing the Anglican church could apply or be extended to the colonies, for the acts of uniformity of 1559 and 1660 did not affect the plantations! "There is nothing in either of these Statutes that so much as looks like a Design of Extending the Establishment to these American Plantations." Mr. Hobart also pointed out that

25. *Boston News-Letter,* January 15, 1741.

the colonies were dominions of the crown—like Guernsey and Jersey, which had belonged to Queen Elizabeth in 1559, and like Ireland for the same reason—Parliament had no authority to legislate for them. This telling constitutional point made by Mr. Hobart for ecclesiastical reasons would be borrowed later by Silas Downer and John Adams and others for use as a political weapon against Parliament.[26]

Many close observers of the provincial scene from the middle of the seventeenth century forward mentioned the deep-flowing republican current in public affairs. Republicanism was most noticeable in religious institutions and had made rapid advances during the religious revolution. There could be little doubt that the majority of the colonists favored it. From Stratford, Connecticut, in 1745, the Reverend Samuel Johnson advised the Bishop of London that: "It has always been a fact, and is obvious in the nature of the thing, that anti-Episcopal are of course anti-monarchical principles. So that the danger of our affecting Independency can never come from a regular Episcopacy, but would naturally flow from the want of it;—from that turbulent outrageous spirit which enthusiasm is apt to inspire men with." Organized religion, it is evident, was not only republican in fact, as well as in spirit, but was also moving in a democratic direction.[27]

The indubitable republicanism of the emerging American mind was buttressed by a well-developed sense of liberty among ordinary people. Writing in 1760 about the Pennsylvanians, Andrew Burnaby sensed this about

26. Noah Hobart, *A Sermon Addressed to the Members of the Episcopal Separation in New-England* (Boston, 1749), 19–24; Hobart, *A Second Address*, 31–37.
27. Samuel Johnson to Edmund Gibson, Bishop of London, November 25, 1745 (Fulham Palace MSS), printed in Arthur L. Cross, *The Anglican Episcopate and the American Colonies* (Cambridge, 1900), 107.

them: "They are great republicans, and have fallen into the same errors in their ideas of independency as most of the other colonies have. As they consist of several nations, and talk several languages, they are aliens in some respect to Great Britain: nor can it be expected that they should have the same filial attachment to her which her own immediate offspring have. . . ." [28]

Years of neglect by English authority had forced the colonists to develop internally in their own—and different—ways. Gradually and unobtrusively the concept of religious liberty, for which the Puritans had crossed the Atlantic on their errand into the wilderness, expanded to embrace civil liberties too. The identity of the law of God and the law of Nature was impressed upon congregations almost weekly by Congregational and Presbyterian ministers. This was the American thing. When the people of Boston rose against authority in 1747 during the Knowles riots, their defense was that when government fails, as it did so signally on that occasion, they were exercising a "Natural Right." This claim was not a novel one, nor was the insistence that "Perhaps there never was a Time when an honest Freedom of Speech was more necessary." One must face the truth that in the forties at Boston, public opinion was expressing the spirit usually assigned to '76. [29]

Before the French and Indian War, the planting gentry of Virginia had had very little connection with the other provinces to the north or to the south, except Maryland. The religious excitement of the times scarcely touched them; they were nominally all Episcopalians and many of them sat on vestries. Nearly all of their relations were with London, from which, however, they too derived

28. Andrew Burnaby, *Travels through the Middle Settlements in North America in the Years 1759 and 1760* (Ithaca, N.Y., 1960), 28.
29. *Independent Advertiser* [Boston], February 8, May 30, 1748.

libertarian ideas and books elucidating them. Long accustomed to managing their internal affairs, the Virginians displayed essentially the same republican attitudes as the northerners. A prolonged visit to the Old Dominion in 1759 led the Reverend Andrew Burnaby, Vicar of Greenwich, to conclude that "the publick or political character of the Virginians, corresponds with their private one: they are haughty and jealous of their liberties, impatient of restraint, and can scarcely bear the thought of being controuled by any superior power. Many of them consider the colonies as independent states, not connected with Great Britain, otherwise than by having the same common king, and being bound to her with natural affection." [30]

Natural affection, however, was being strained, and resentment was taking its place. Outstanding among the grievances that the aristocrats of the Old Dominion held against the mother country was her interference with its laws. After two years of painstaking work, in 1748 the Assembly completed a revision of the legal code, which, as usual, was sent over to Whitehall for royal approval. There were sixty-seven acts in all; on April 8, 1752, four years later, Governor Dinwiddie announced that ten of them had been disallowed by the Privy Council. Here was outside interference with the very essence of self-government. As John Mercer of Spotsylvania told the House of Burgesses: "it is a very difficult matter to distinguish which . . . Acts are in Force and which are not." From this time forward, indignation, if not anger, against the mother country spread and gradually the Virginians grew to understand that they shared the common lot of all Americans. [31]

30. Burnaby, *Travels*, 24.
31. *Journal of the House of Burgesses of Virginia, 1758–1761*, ed. H. R. McIlwaine (Richmond, 1908), 136.

The tiny village of Jamestown in Virginia could have celebrated a sesquicentennial in 1757, and three of the leading seaboard cities—New York, Boston, and Newport—had long since passed the century mark. The dynamic expansion of the colonies, coupled with material improvements of every kind known to the age enabled the million-and-a-half inhabitants to have closer and more frequent exchanges with each other. During the French wars and religious revivals, profound changes in sentiments and feelings had come about, and an American public opinion was forming that, in some respects, had already superseded some provincial attitudes, an opinion that was especially observable in a universal optimism and self-confidence. On the other hand, the colonists entertained mixed emotions about their English rulers. These sensations they allowed to go unvoiced for the most part, and whether they would forget their grievances and resentments depended on what the future would bring.

IV
Patriotism Described and Recommended
1760-1770

A number of seemingly unrelated incidents of the year 1760 illustrates how disparate were the elements that went into the maturing sentiment for American unity during the last years of the colonial period. At Boston on the night of March 20, the most disastrous fire ever experienced on this continent destroyed four hundred structures and caused the loss of more than £100,000 sterling to its inhabitants. One can scarcely imagine a more instructive example of the growing popular sympathy for the welfare of all Americans than the promptness and generosity displayed by individuals, churches, towns, and public bodies up and down the entire coast as far away as Charleston in contributing the large sum of £13,317.11.9 for the relief of 439 "sufferers."

In the oldest dominion of the crown, the planting gentry and the Episcopalian clergy were engaged in a contest, known as the Parson's Cause, over an emergency act passed by the House of Burgesses. The act had been one of ten disallowed in 1752, for it had not contained a clause suspending its operation until royal approval was given. In this year, 1760, one of the most conservative

members of the aristocratic legislature opened the constitutional issue to public discussion when he argued in *A
Letter to the Clergy of Virginia* that the governor and council should regard the public good as the highest law and,
"where this Necessity prevails, every Consideration must
give Place to it"; even royal instructions "may be de-
viated from with Impunity." [1]

Peace negotiations had been going on in Paris for several months before the fall of Montreal on September 8,
1760, which brought the last French War to an end on
this continent and what was popularly called "the Gallic
peril" passed into history. More than one French states-
man recognized at once what the removal of this century-
old menace could mean to the victorious nation. His
most Christian Majesty's ambassador to the Sublime
Porte, the Comte de Vergennes, remarked to an English
acquaintance at Constantinople: "You are happy in the
cession of Canada: we, perhaps, ought to think ourselves
happy that you have acquired it. Delivered from a neigh-
bour whom they have always feared, your other colonies
will soon discover, that they stand no longer in need of
your protection. You will call on them to contribute toward supporting the burthen which they have helped to
bring on you, they will answer you by shaking off all
dependence." [2]

In April, at London, Benjamin Franklin published a
tract, which quickly became famous, entitled *The Interest*

1. Richard Bland, *A Letter to the Clergy of Virginia* (Williamsburg,
   1760), 18; and the important elaboration of his constitutional argument for the exclusive power of the assembly to make all laws "for
   the Internal Government of the Colony" in *The Colonel Dismounted,
   or the Rector Vindicated* (Williamsburg, 1764), 21, 23.
2. [John Lind], *Three Letters to Dr. Price, Containing Remarks on His Observations on the Nature of Civil Liberty* (London, 1776), 136–37n.;
   [George Chalmers], *Second Thoughts or Observations upon Lord Abing-
   don's Thoughts on the Letter of Edmund Burke to the Sheriffs of Bristol*, 2d
   ed. (London, 1777), 71–72.

of Great Britain Considered in which he called for the retention of captured Canada in the peace settlement. "I hope it will appear before I end these sheets," he wrote, "that if ever there was a *national war,* this is truly such a one: a war in which the interest of the *whole* nation is directly and fundamentally concerned." Here spoke the British imperialist, who within a few months would applaud the accession of the third Hanoverian to the throne (October 25) and, early in the next year, heartily approve of the round of joyous celebrations of that event by the citizens of the principal colonial seaports. However, in 1768, Franklin would be privately expressing the most serious doubts about the authority of Parliament to regulate the colonies and eventually would refer to Great Britain as "this rotten old State." Writing from London on February 18, 1774, to John Foxcroft, the deputy postmaster in New York, the sage of Philadelphia advised him that "It seems I am too much of an American. Take care of yourself for you are little less." [3]

As King George III opened his reign, the colonists' outlook in the two great spheres of agriculture and commerce appeared more than favorable. What is known today as economic growth had been proceeding at a most rapid pace with the obvious result that the English provinces on the North American continent were lashed together more tightly and irrevocably than ever before. The removal of both the French and Spanish threats to English security by the Paris treaties of 1763 and the creation of the new provinces of East and West Florida and Quebec extended the domain of colonial coastal commerce all the way from Montreal to Pensacola at the

3. *The Papers of Benjamin Franklin,* ed. Leonard W. Labaree (New Haven, 1966), IX, 75; *The Writings of Benjamin Franklin,* ed. Albert H. Smyth (New York, 1906), VI, 198.

same time that vast, apparently limitless tracts of land for settlement became available as far west as the Mississippi River.

During the years following 1760 a phenomenal growth of population took place in the colonies: the number of native-born whites doubled and was continually supplemented by a large immigration of Scotch-Irish and Palatines and the importation of many slaves. When the thirteen colonies declared their independence in 1776, they contained an estimated 2,500,000 to 2,600,000 inhabitants, 500,000 of whom were blacks. One of the "Wonders of the World," as contemporaries averred, was the urban development along the Atlantic seaboard, which the newspapers mirrored in a hundred ways. The five largest cities—Philadelphia, New York, Boston, Charleston, and Newport—numbered about 104,000 people in 1775; and fifteen growing secondary port towns contained about 77,012, making a total urban population of around 181,012.

Merchants and shippers of these seaports conducted a notable expansion of imports, as well as the exports to pay for them. Imports of British manufactures, especially luxury items desired by city dwellers and southern planters, were rapidly mounting; in 1772, according to Burke, £6,024,000 worth of British goods went to the colonists as compared with £485,000 to other customers. The colonial export trade with the sugar islands of the Caribbean was increasing as was that with the Wine Islands, some Mediterranean countries, and West Africa. A newly developed and highly profitable maritime venture was whaling (the hardihood displayed in the prosecution of this fishery fascinated Edmund Burke). Matching the growth of overseas shipping was an equally significant extension of the coastal traffic for collecting and distributing goods and produce. By 1765 coal from the falls of the James River in Virginia was being shipped out, and Gerrard Ellison was advertising its value for blacksmiths in the newspapers of Philadelphia and Newport. Two years later one could make trips on schedule between Charleston and Pensacola on the "Grenville Pacquet-Boat." [4]

Improvements in travel and inland communications from the four largest cities, in some respects, were more important than those for the water-borne commerce just mentioned. Better highways, bridges, more and faster postal service, and proposals for canals were desired by the people of the back parts, and in order to implement these "internal improvements," they had to look beyond provincial boundaries: in 1761 a committee to arrange for the building of a stone church and market house in the great Valley of Virginia at Winchester sought bids for the job through the *Pennsylvania Gazette*. The spread of settlement in the Back Country had made Philadelphia second only to London in all of the king's dominions "in the scale of exportations," wrote "Publicola," but he added a warning about potential competition from Baltimore and other Maryland ports. So impressive were the advances made in coastwise and interior communications and economic exchange that the interdependence they created proved to be the most powerful single factor binding the colonists together, not merely by commercial bonds, but religiously and socially as well. [5]

Everywhere wealth accumulated as the settlers brought additional acreages under cultivation. To meet the complex requirements of the growing population, the

4. *Pennsylvania Gazette*, October 3, 1765; *Pennsylvania Chronicle*, July 20, 1767.
5. See, in this connection especially, the fine work of Henry Mouzon and others, *An Accurate Map of North and South Carolina With Their Indian Frontiers* (London, 1775). *Pennsylvania Gazette*, April 16, 1761; *Pennsylvania Chronicle*, January 26, 1767.

number and variety of artisans and craftsmen rose, and such industries as shipbuilding, the manufacture of iron and lumber products, coal mining, and lime-burning grew profitable. In the cities men had sums of money to lend or invest, often in thousands of pounds. When Colonel John Chiswell, sorely in need of ready money, could not get a loan in Virginia, he solicited one for £2000 from the leading magnate of Pennsylvania, Chief Justice Allen, only to learn that "we have among us ten Borrowers to one Lender." What is significant is the existence of intercolonial money-lending as early as the period of the French and Indian War.[6]

In nearly every respect, land continued to be the primary source of wealth, and the visible fact, as Lord Adam Gordon observed about Massachusetts in 1765, was that "the levelling principle . . . every where operates strongly, and takes the lead, and every body has property, and every body knows it"; a larger proportion of the inhabitants owned some land (possessed real property in fee simple) than anywhere else in the world. What with the evidences of material progress all about them, it is small wonder that the American colonies had developed a great love for and a deep-seated faith in their country and hope of a prosperous future.[7]

In spite of obvious growth and well-being, dark clouds loomed on the horizon that made more than a few men uneasy and filled them with forebodings. Serious obstacles to a maturing and thriving economy existed in 1760, and in the succeeding years of this period, others were added. Adjustment to a normal existence after a

6. *The Burd Papers: Extracts from Chief Justice William Allen's Letter Book*, ed. Lewis B. Walker (Pottsville, Pa., 1897), 16.

7. Lord Adam Gordon, "Travels in North America . . . in 1764–1765," in *Travels in the American Colonies*, ed. Newton D. Mereness (New York, 1916), 451.

long and severe war is always difficult. The change-over to peace, beginning in 1762 with the departure of the British troops for the Caribbean, brought to an end the flow of hard money they had pumped into the economy and lucrative war contracts also came to an end. As the year ended the contraction of the colonial economy and the shortage of money had produced a full-fledged depression, which was deepened by the British authorities forbidding the issuance of paper currency. Provincial war debts and taxes levied to pay them, as well as high local taxes at Boston and Newport, produced genuine distress in Massachusetts and Rhode Island and intensified the postwar depression, which, as we know today, was widespread in the colonies by 1762 and lasted, with ups and downs, for many citizens in the towns up to 1775.

Financial problems were indeed critical and were made more difficult because all of the credit and banking facilities for the economy were centered in London. The long line of credit extended from the London merchant to the colonial merchant, factor, or planter; and from them to the country storekeeper, city small shopkeeper, the peddler, and on to the ultimate consumer on the farm or in the town. Credit allowances at each stage were not infrequently for two years; and when the English merchant pressed for payment, every colonial along the line felt the weight of it.

Financial stringency was, perhaps, felt in Virginia more widely than elsewhere, for the tobacco planters were on the verge of bankruptcy. The son-in-law of John Chiswell, Speaker John Robinson, who was also treasurer of the province, felt that the colony itself would suffer grievously if the aristocrats were ruined. To rescue them, he evolved the scheme of taking bills of credit that came to him for redemption and, instead of destroying them, used them to bail out his old friends. Over a period of three years he gave out £100,761, a process that was not publicly known until after his death when more than a hundred of the borrowers still owed large sums to his estate.[8]

The hard times bore severely on the middle and lower class townsfolk, who, unlike the farmers, had no land to fall back on for subsistence. Artisans, tradesmen, journeymen, craftsmen, boatmen, and longshoremen were all hit in one way or another, an experience that eventually every colonial could understand. Reports of great merchants, as well as small tradesmen, failing and of foreclosures on properties were so noised about that it is not surprising that the anomaly of imprisonment for debt became a favorite topic of conversation at urban taverns. Men, bewildered and helpless, allowed their emotions to triumph over reason.

Whether the times were good or bad, all of the colonists had come to realize the dependence of one region upon another, and the appearance of voluntary associations of intercolonial scope, nearly all of which have survived, bears this out. An interesting fact about these associations, and single meetings or events of more than local appeal, is the conscious use of the word *American* in many of the titles. The colonists heard or learned of the events or organizations from the pulpit, in tavern discussions, in conversation, on the highroads, or read about them in tracts or newspapers of the time. Ecclesiastical bodies had been in existence for a long time, and their leaders had devised methods that, considering the age and state of communications, had proved amazingly efficient in propagating and protecting their religious

8. For lists of the debtors to the Robinson Estate in 1766 and 1792, see Appendixes II–VI in the definitive account by David J. Mays, in *Edmund Pendleton: 1721–1802* (Cambridge, 1952), I, 142–55, 174–208, 358–85.

rights. Members of all the largest religious bodies—
Quakers, Baptists, Presbyterians, German Reformed,
Lutherans, and Episcopalians—could be found in nearly
every province, and most of them looked upon Philadelphia as their denominational capital. The Congregationalists were spread all over New England and had
adherents in South Carolina. Furthermore they had
maintained relations in the colonies and in Britain and on
the continent of Europe with Presbyterians and other
Calvinist groups.

The following list of organizations and events compiled from newspaper notices of this period gives eloquent testimony of intercolonial bonds.

1761   The United Company of Spermaceti Chandlers (in
        1763 included Boston, Providence, Newport, and
        Philadelphia manufacturers).

1763   David Douglass's Players take the name of "The
        American Company of Comedians," and perform
        in South Carolina, Virginia, Maryland, Pennsyl-
        vania, New York, and Rhode Island; also in West
        Indies.

1765   The Sons of Liberty develop an intercolonial orga-
        nization to oppose the Stamp Act: Massachusetts,
        Rhode Island, Connecticut, New York, Pennsyl-
        vania, Maryland, South Carolina.

1767–   Annual Convention of Delegates of the Presby-
1775   terian and Consociated Congregational Churches of
        Connecticut to protect religious liberties: New Eng-
        land, New York, New Jersey, Pennsylvania.

1768   The American Society, held at Philadelphia, for
        promoting Useful Knowledge.

        June 21: "This Day may be considered as having
        given Birth to Medical Honors in America"—
        College of Philadelphia confers first degrees of

Bachelor of medicine upon ten graduates from Pennsylvania, Delaware, and New Jersey.

Patrick and Thomas Kennedy advertise in the *Pennsylvania Chronicle* for "Lovers of art and their country" to sell at their print shop "elegant gardens, landscapes, and AMERICAN VIEWS, fit for Gentlemen FARMERS," and Robert Bell of Philadelphia had for sale "an elegant engraved Copperplate Print of the Patriotic American Farmer" [John Dickinson], glazed and framed, for five shillings.[9]

1769 January 2. First meeting of the united American Philosophical Society, Held at Philadelphia, for promoting Useful Knowledge.

Observation of the Transit of Venus by members of this Society at Philadelphia, Lewes, Providence, Newport, and in New Jersey.[10]

Society of Dissenters, consisting of laymen opposed to Episcopacy, organized in New York City, and soliciting intercolonial, English, and Scottish members.[11]

Lewis Nicola published the first Transactions of the American Philosophical Society in his *American Magazine*.[12]

1771 American Medical Society founded at Philadelphia.[13]

Society for promoting Learning amongst the Baptist Churches [in America].[14]

9. *Pennsylvania Chronicle*, June 27, October 24, December 12, 1768.
10. *Pennsylvania Gazette*, June 8, 1769.
11. *Pennsylvania Chronicle*, October 9, 1769.
12. Early in 1769, Lewis Nicola began to publish *The American Magazine*, and as an appendix to the monthly issues from February to September, he included the early transactions of the two bodies that formed the united society that year. These have been reprinted in facsimile as Volume LXXVII of the *Memoirs of the American Philosophical Society* (Philadelphia, 1969).
13. *Pennsylvania Packet*, November 2, 1772.
14. *Pennsylvania Chronicle*, September 9, 1771.

Transactions of the American Philosophical Society, published for continental and European distribution.[15]

Robert Bell, Philadelphia bookseller, undertakes first "national advertising" by seeking through most of the newspapers, subscriptions for his edition of Blackstone's *Commentaries* from "all those who are animated by the wish of seeing Native Fabrications flourish in America." [16]

1772   Sons of St. Tammany organized at New York by "a Number of Americans" to promote charity and be of "Utility to the Distressed." [17]

1773   The American Society for promoting Religious Knowledge Among the Poor in the British Colonies prints its rules.[18]

"Proposals for Printing, A Splendid Edition of a new work, entitled the American Genealogist: in which a particular account will be given of the origin, progress, intermarriages, etc. of most of the considerable families in America.[19]

Formation of "Fellows of the American Society of Language" proposed at Boston and Portsmouth to "the Literati of America" for "the perfecting the English Language in America." [20]

The return to normal times and everyday activities so much anticipated did not take place in 1760 nor for a

15. *Pennsylvania Chronicle*, September 23, 1771; *Boston Gazette*, October 7, 1771.
16. *Pennsylvania Packet*, October 28, 1771.
17. *Pennsylvania Chronicle*, May 4, 11, 1772.
18. *Pennsylvania Packet*, August 9, 1773; *Pennsylvania Journal*, November 10, 1773.
19. This proposal may have been made in jest, but in any event it pointed to the distinction accruing to families that had been in America for several generations. *Pennsylvania Packet*, November 22, 1773.
20. *Royal American Magazine* [Boston], I, 6–7; *New Hampshire Gazette*, April 22, 1774.

long time thereafter. Growth was continually hampered and periodically interrupted, if not deliberately delayed, by the political actions of Parliament and the efforts of royal officials to tighten control over the colonies or, in effect, to reorder the British Empire by centralizing it in new and unconstitutional ways. Startled at first by these actions taken at Whitehall and Westminster, the colonists proceeded to investigate the precise nature of their connection with Great Britain and, for the first time, to assess its value publicly; and before a decade had passed the issues were drawn.

Too much emphasis cannot be laid on the fact that sooner or later there was something in British policy that directly affected, or seemed to threaten, the religious or political liberties of every individual in the English colonies. Each successive step toward further commercial and political control by authority external to the colonial assemblies was apparently accompanied by parallel proposals to extend ecclesiastical control. This almost rhythmic or periodic sequence of external regulations and piling up of events during the sixties induced a situation that was highly charged with emotion. The emotionalism was no longer merely an intermittent intercolonial expression of fears about a possible loss of religious liberties and long-exercised rights of civil government. It was lasting and it was American.

Americanism was still something the average man felt only deep within himself, something that words could not describe. A greater number of people than ever before were thinking about the issues, and the printers were publishing their doubts and conclusions for all to read. To contemporaries, of course, their experience was like a single rope: no one thought of raveling it in order to inspect the separate strands of religion, economics, politics, patriotism, or public opinion. Still, for present purposes, an examination of some of these strands separately should aid us to grasp what men thought and how they felt—the Spirit of '76.

The sustained secular drift of our own times must not be permitted through sheer ignorance or cynicism to black out of history the potent fact that religion was the central concern for most Americans, not only throughout the entire century and a half of settlement on this continent but of the era of the Revolution as well. Who can deny that for them the very core of existence was their relation to God? Between 1762 and 1770, a great proportion of them suffered unrelieved apprehensions because hard-won republican concepts and practices of church polity were being seriously menaced by the proposed extensions of control by the Church of England to the colonies. Both the S. P. G. missionaries of the middle and New England colonies, and Thomas Secker, Archbishop of Canterbury, took steps between 1762 and 1766 to persuade royal political and ecclesiastical authorities to create an Anglican episcopate in America by sending one or more bishops overseas. It did not take long, however, for the excellent intelligence agents of the Congregationalists to learn of these intentions and to have the scheme thoroughly aired in the London and colonial papers. No less an eminent personage than the Reverend George Whitefield gravely warned two prominent ministers at Portsmouth, New Hampshire, in April 1764: "There is a deep laid plot against both your civil and religious liberties, and they will be lost. Your golden days are at an end." [21]

When the Grenville reform program took effect in

21. Quoted by William Gordon in *The History of the Rise, Progress, and Establishment of the United States of America* (London, 1788), I, 143–48.

1764 and 1765, many colonials had come to the conclusion that the Sugar, Currency, and Stamp acts and the plan for a bishop were all part of one concerted plan. The appearance in the *Boston Gazette*, commencing on August 12, 1765, of four masterly essays elaborated the dangers inherent in a fusing of the civil and canon laws, which the colonists had so far escaped. The anonymous author, revealed as John Adams in 1770, urged all printers to spread the news of this imminent catastrophe throughout the land. Obviously he accepted the idea of a conspiracy to subvert American liberties and sought to link civil and religious tyranny in the minds of his readers. Concurrently the activities of the S. P. G. missionaries as the only prominent group of colonial leaders to support the Stamp Act lent credence to the charge of a plot; these Anglican missionaries became the nucleus of the Tory party.

Surprising as it may seem, one of the most penetrating estimates of the temper of the times came from an S. P. G. missionary in South Carolina. The Reverend Charles Martin warned the Bishop of London in October 1765: "The Principles of most of the Colonists in America are independent in Matters of Religion, as well as republican in those of Government: and if I may form a Judgment from the prevailing turbulent Spirit, which like an Epidemic Disorder seems every where to diffuse itself thro' this and other Colonies, I can venture to affirm that it wou'd be as unsafe for an American Bishop (if such should be appointed) to come hither, as it is at present to a Distributor of Stamps." Weighty support for the view that the threats to liberties were both religious and civil were not imaginary also came from London: looking back after the repeal of the Stamp Act, a writer stated flatly in 1766 in the *St. James's Chronicle* that "the Stamping and Episcopizing our Colonies were understood to be only different Branches of the same Plan of Power." [22]

The repeal of the Stamp Act in March 1766 was followed closely by the Declaratory Act in which the right of Parliament to make all laws necessary to bind the colonies was asserted "in all cases whatsoever," and shortly after came another drive on both sides of the water to establish an episcopate. For all but a few Episcopalian clergymen of the northern colonies, the next four years were a period of great fear during which a bitter struggle developed between the proponents of the Church of England and the far more numerous Presbyterians, Dutch Reformed, and the Lutherans in New York over the demands of these so-called "dissenters" for incorporation; the contest finally ended in a victory for the Anglicans.

During these four years the Presbyterians and Congregationalists successfully conducted newspaper and pamphlet campaigns at New York and Philadelphia to guard against any popular misconception of what episcopacy would entail if it were introduced into the colonies. According to a *Boston Chronicle* of 1767, there were at least 550 ministers, most of them of the Congregational persuasion and graduates of one or another of the colonial colleges, serving in New England; and in New York there were 155 ministers: 96 divided among the "dissenters"; 38 Quakers and 21 Anglicans.[23]

The members of "Mr. Otis's black Regiment, the dissenting clergy," improved the opportunity they enjoyed weekly to indoctrinate their listeners with Americanism

22. Rev. Charles Martin to the Bishop of London, October 20, 1765, Fulham Palace MSS (Library of Congress Transcripts), South Carolina, no. 320; *St. James's Chronicle* [London], June 14, 1766.
23. *Boston Chronicle*, December 28, 1767; *Pennsylvania Chronicle*, March 16, 1767.

as they had earlier taught them the history of the errand into the wilderness, and to elucidate the nature of religious and civil liberties. Jonathan Mayhew performed his greatest service as an American, rather than as a minister, by suggesting to James Otis in June 1766 that the politicians take over the effective device of committees of correspondence, which the ministers had used for almost a century with great success. Adopted as a weapon against "tyranny," these "eggs of sedition," as Daniel Leonard branded them, were fashioned into potent engines of revolutionary action. The ministers also pointed a way to American unity when the Presbyterians of the middle and southern provinces and the Consociated Congregational Churches of Connecticut arranged to convene an annual Convention of Delegates specifically aimed at the preservation of their mutual religious liberties. Its first full meeting took place at Elizabeth Town in New Jersey in September 1766, and the delegates continued to forgather until independence rendered their liberties secure. In a very real sense, these meetings foreshadowed those of the continental congresses.[24]

In a public address made in 1768, and soon published, Silas Downer, a Providence lawyer and one of the most active and determined of all the Sons of Liberty, used the distinction made by the Reverend Noah Hobart in 1752 between the realm and the dominions that totally repudiated the Declaratory Act on the ground that Parliament

24. Jonathan Mayhew to James Otis, June 8, 1766, printed in Alden Bradford, *Memoir of the Life and Writings of the Rev. Jonathan Mayhew* (Boston, 1838), 428–30. *Peter Oliver's Origin and Progress of the American Revolution* [1781], ed. Douglass Adair and John A. Schutz (San Marino, Calif., 1961), especially pp. 29, 41–45; *Minutes of the Convention of Delegates from the Synod of New York and Philadelphia, and from the Associations of Connecticut; Held Annually from 1766 to 1775 Inclusive* (Hartford, 1843), 8–17.

could act only for "the common People of Britain." A year later a merchant at Manhattan received a letter on July 20 from a gentleman living in one of the interior towns of New York, which revealed the complete merging in public thinking of ideas about economic, civil, and religious liberties. In cautioning the merchant not to import any more English goods, the writer states that he was present at several town meetings at which resolutions were passed to this effect: (1) that to purchase any Scottish or English manufacturers from merchants was "in fact a sure wicked way to qualify Britain tyrannically and inflexibly, from time to time to impose upon Americans, whatsoever new laws, new admiralty courts, or Bishops Courts they pleased to take away our civil and religious liberties piece-meal," and (2) anyone buying British goods is to be considered an "open enemy to all civil and religious interests of their country." A group of laymen in the city of New York formed a Society of Dissenters and sought a continental membership to protect religious rights.[25]

About this same time, at Norwich, the ministers of the General Association of Connecticut referred fervently in their proceedings to "the dark and threatening Aspect of divine Providence upon our Nation and Land in regard to their civil Liberties and public Interest." Perhaps it was a divine providence that took Archbishop Secker from this earthly scene and thereby permitted the issue of episcopacy to wither away. Its last flurry occurred among the established clergy of the Old Dominion in 1770 and 1771 when a large majority of them rejected the idea of a bishop out-of-hand inasmuch as they had long been accustomed to lax discipline and dealing with "con-

25. Silas Downer's *A Discourse* is reprinted in Carl Bridenbaugh, *Silas Downer: Forgotten Patriot, His Life and Writings* (Providence, 1974), 99–113; *Pennsylvania Journal*, August 3, 1769.

gregational vestries." For this action, the House of Burgesses, most of whom were vestrymen, voted its thanks.[26]

In this discussion the usual order of treating politics ahead of religion has been deliberately reversed; yet this is permissible, for from the very beginning of American history religion took precedence. Politics is, after all, always an end product, an overt component of silent and long-operating forces. It is effect rather more often than a cause. It has also been evident that some of the most useful modes of organizing the revolutionary movement were borrowed from tried and true ecclesiastical precedents. In the middle colonies and New England the ministers worked hand-in-glove with the political leaders. Because the focus in these pages is on the people and their quickening awareness of American unity, it will be well to inquire into some special political incidents that contributed particularly to the emotional responses.

Among the ordinary colonists in 1760, possession and enjoyment of some real property was widespread. Not a few artisans and tradesmen of the towns and even an occasional carter and boatman owned the houses in which they lived. For those not so fortunate, the hope that sometime they might acquire land and a house was far from chimerical. From many of these people, however, the postwar depression swept away any such dreams: failures in the crafts and trades were many, the newspapers carried the sad stories of numerous foreclosures, and as shipping and shipbuilding declined, unemployment rose among sailors and mechanics. In certain colonies, especially Massachusetts and Rhode Island, provincial taxes, and local too, were so high that many persons

26. *Records of the General Association of the Colony of Connecticut* (Hartford, 1888), 66–67; *Pennsylvania Chronicle*, August 5, 1771.

became delinquent, as Samuel Adams, a collector, knew only too well. Loss of land or other property or jobs was a very real experience for many urban and rural Americans.

In Virginia the tobacco gentry had passed its peak economically, and the members of the House of Burgesses had grown almost fiercely resentful over outside interference with the internal government of the largest colony. In no area of the planting interest was this sensitivity more evident than in the matter of finance and taxation, as Richard Bland made clear in 1760 in *A Letter to the Clergy of Virginia* dealing with the Two-Penny Act and four years later in *The Colonel Dismounted*. An indication of how fortunes stood with the small tobacco growers was the statement of John Dickinson in 1765 that Virginia sheriffs, "instead of raising the annual levies, have been obliged to make returns into the treasury of effects which they have taken in execution, but could not sell, as there were no bidders for ready money." [27]

The incidence of the Sugar and Currency acts upon the trading centers of Boston, Newport, and Providence caused genuine distress. Writing anonymously in the *Providence Gazette* in 1764, Silas Downer described sardonically the objectives of the new colonial policy: "*America* can answer all expences of government, and afford a certain fund for supporting as many *Mother-Countrymen*, as ought to be maintained from *America*, in consideration of their being born in *Britain*." In October of this year, Joseph Harrison, Yorkshire-born merchant of Newport, sailed from New London bearing a petition for the crown to resume the charters of "the two Republicks

---

27. John Dickinson, *The Late Regulations Respecting the British Colonies* (Philadelphia, 1765), 18n.; also reprinted by Bernard Bailyn in *Pamphlets of the American Revolution* (Cambridge, 1965), I, 679n.

of Connecticut and Rhode Island" and possibly of Massachusetts, and also a "new Arrangement of New England" along the lines of a scheme concurrently proposed by Governor Francis Bernard of the Bay Colony addressed to Lord Halifax. Both parties contemplated a civil list of British-born officials (like Harrison) supported by colonial customs or tax revenues; and in addition Bernard wanted to eliminate "the republican cast" by creating a nobility for life to act as "a third legislative power" independent of the people. The small clique of "foreigners" who engineered the mission thought it was known only to themselves, but the details leaked out and were bruited about by grapevine and newspapers throughout Connecticut, Rhode Island, and Massachusetts. If the readers of the *Providence Gazette* needed any proof of a plot to subvert their government, this incident provided it in full measure.[28]

In his *Dissertation on the Feudal and Canon Law* published in 1765, John Adams analyzed the earlier contest in Britain against civil and spiritual tyranny: "It was this great struggle that peopled America. It was not religion alone, as is commonly supposed; but it was a love of universal liberty, and a hatred, a dread, a horror, of the infernal confederacy before described, that projected, conducted, and accomplished the settlement of America." The publication of such works as this by John Adams, which reached a large audience through the newspapers, the Stamp Act riots, in which bloodshed and outright rebellion were narrowly averted, and the constant barrage of dialectics by Congregational and Presbyterian

28. *Providence Gazette*, August 18, 1764, reprinted in Bridenbaugh, *Silas Downer*, 71–72; Francis Bernard to Lord Halifax, November 9, 1764, Bernard Papers, X, 238–43, in Sparks MSS, IV (Houghton Library, Harvard University).

ministers were disseminating the seeds of the Spirit of '76 so far and wide that, before long, the point of no return would be reached.[29]

The salient feature, or blunder, of the Stamp Act was that it affected all regions and nearly every member of the colonies in one way or another, particularly the most vocal elements—the printers, lawyers, and members of the several assemblies. An uproar rose throughout the land upon the announcement of the stamp duties. In Virginia, for example, "A general alarm . . . and universal consternation" prevailed, and James Maury advised John Fontaine on December 31, 1765, that if some critics brand us as "rebels," others "may applaud us for that generous *love of liberty* which we inherit from *our glorious forefathers* . . . If the Parliament indeed have a right to impose taxes on the colonies, we are as absolute slaves as any in Asia, and consequently in a state of rebellion . . . The people of Virginia conclude, *the Parliament have no right to tax them.*" [30]

Although the outstanding public opposition to the detested bill was the calling of the Stamp Act Congress at New York, far more effective was the sub rosa forming of local bodies of citizens, largely middle class, who called themselves Sons of Liberty, and the beginnings of a continental organization by means of covert committees of correspondence. The Sons were behind the August riots in Boston and helped to promote disturbances at Newport. Governor William Bull of South Carolina thought that the stamp duties would have been paid and the Charlestonians satisfied with peaceable protests "but

29. *The Works of John Adams*, ed. Charles Francis Adams (Boston, 1851), III, 451.
30. Ann Maury, *Memoirs of a Huguenot Family* (New York, 1853), 424–30 (my italics).

by the artifices of some busy Spirits the Minds of men here were so universally poisoned with the Principles which were imbitered and propagated from Boston and Rhode Island (from which Towns, at this time of the Year, Vessels very frequently arrive) that after their example the People . . . resolved to seize and destroy the Stamp Papers." [31]

An example of how news originated and circulated is a letter sent to London from Boston (dated August 22, 1765, just before the Stamp Act riots) to the printer of the *Public Advertiser*, who published it. On December 23, 1765, Solomon Southwick ran an extract of it in the *Newport Mercury*: "Did we not second your designs in your unmeaning expedition to Carthagena, by sending 4000 men thither; which you there used up? Or have you forgot our giving you a peace by taking Cape-Breton in 1745. The successes that we gave you at Martinico are too recent to have escaped your memory: And if the North Americans had not seasonably arrived at Havannah when a raging distemper carried off your troops 'tis presumed the place could not have been taken. 'Tis true you took Quebec, in conjunction with the Royal Americans, who during the war had above 15,000 men in the field. Now you, on your side of the water, make a merit of taking Canada for our sakes;—but you know better,—and that it was for your own sakes." The reward for all of these sacrifices and services, the writer continues, was taxes, and by sending over jailbirds who infest the road from New York to Philadelphia, making it worse than Hounslow Heath. "Such are some of the precious returns from our Indulgent parent, for our many services."

31. William Bull to Lords of Trade and Plantations, November 3, 1765, George Chalmers, Papers relating to Carolina (New York Public Library), I, 175.

Though not altogether accurate reporting, the item served to evoke old memories and helped to make many a colonist more of an American than ever before.[32]

The able and observant servant of the crown, Francis Bernard, reported to the Lords of Trade and Plantations in August 1766 that the proper internal constitution of Massachusetts had been badly deranged since the Stamp Act troubles. "The popular leaders have laboured so successfully, that the very principles of the common people have changed; and they now form to themselves pretensions and expectations which had never entered their heads a year or two ago." And this held just as true in other provinces. Everywhere the attitudes and activities of the Sons displayed a sense of unity, and they evinced very little respect for or loyalty to the British monarchy.[33]

The repeal of the odious Stamp Act in 1766, while applauded by many people, including some Sons of Liberty, was looked upon by Silas Downer and some other shrewd observers of the political scene as an act of expediency rather than a recognition of an unpolitic violation of the constitution of the empire. The Declaratory Act, which followed immediately upon the repeal, was cited as proof that there had been no change in policy on the part of the authorities in Britain. As Silas Downer advised his fellow Rhode Islanders through the *Providence Gazette*, the real reason for repealing the Stamp Act was "the Inability of the Government to carry it into Execution." The threat to their liberties seemed as great as ever to him, and he continued to work tirelessly, always undercover, to maintain the correspondence between and

32. *Newport Mercury*, December 23, 1765.
33. Governor Bernard to Lords of Trade and Plantations, August 1768, George Chalmers, Papers relating to New England, II, 14, in Sparks MSS (Houghton Library).

among the Sons, at least as far south as Philadelphia, urging them to keep their organizations intact and alert to counter any future attacks on their civil and religious liberties.[34]

The year 1768 was crowded with events that contributed to overt expressions of the American spirit. The Townshend Acts, the augmented severity of revenue regulations, the meeting of the Convention of Delegates of "dissenting" bodies, the sending of troops to Boston in peacetime were but some of the events of these crowded twelve months that alarmed and agitated the colonists. In England Sir George Saville commented in July to his political chief, the Marquis of Rockingham, ". . . Tis a very melancholy story: I am afraid these same Colonists are above our hands, and I am almost ready to think that G[eorge] G[renville]'s act only brought on a crisis 20 or possibly 50 years sooner than was necessary. This indeed is, regarding the Colonies almost all the ill that can be done, for in my opinion (which may be in that a little irregular) it is in the nature of things that some time or other Colonies so situated must assume to themselves the rights of nature and resist those of the Law, which is Rebellion. By *rights* of nature I mean advantages of situation or their natural *powers.*" This prophetic statement by the man often called the perfect English gentleman was, unfortunately, neither widely circulated nor influential.[35]

Across the Atlantic in Providence on July 25 of that same year, Silas Downer delivered an oration from the summer-house in the Tree of Liberty to an assemblage of several thousand Yankee auditors from Rhode Island,

34. *Providence Gazette*, August 23, 30, 1766; Silas Downer to New York Sons of Liberty, July 1766, printed in Bridenbaugh, *Silas Downer,* 87–95.

35. Sir George Saville to Lord Rockingham, July 31, 1768, Rockingham MSS, in Wentworth-Woodhouse Papers (University of Sheffield, England).

Connecticut, and Massachusetts. The address was published almost at once for all to read as *A Discourse, Delivered at Providence . . . By a Son of Liberty*. In it, Downer set forth publicly, for the first time, the fundamental issues. He told his audience that Parliament did not have and never did have any legislative power over Rhode Island or any other colony. He said many things with impunity that even the most courageous leaders of Massachusetts, Pennsylvania, or Virginia dared not write or even mention publicly, and his listeners, indoctrinated in past years by ministers, newspaper writers, and in public discussions, were prepared for them. They were neither shocked nor startled. Certainly no one went away with any doubts as to what his liberties were or that he was in danger of losing them; he had just listened to a remarkably clear and decisive exposition by a patriot that was intended not just for provincial ears but for American ears.[36]

By the close of the year 1768, in view of the refusal of the ministry to listen to American opinions and the use of troops at Boston, it had become abundantly manifest to the mass of the people—in the southern and middle colonies as well as New England—that the British authorities had no intention of making any accommodation with them. Instead it looked as if Parliament planned to reorder the empire radically without any regard to colonial rights. The Declaratory Act was very specific in asserting Parliament's right to legislate in every field relating to colonial existence, and nothing occurred in the next six or seven years to reverse this position or to revive the hope that colonials might again live assured that self-government through their assemblies would no longer be in jeopardy. What did happen was that a grow-

36. Downer, *A Discourse*, in Bridenbaugh, *Silas Downer*, 99–113.

ing number of able leaders joined John Adams, Silas
Downer, and Richard Bland in their belief that there was
a plot to stifle these colonial governments, and that a substantial body of people in all walks of colonial life acknowledged, however reluctantly, that above all else they
were Americans.

Patriotism, American nationalism—call it what you
will—had as its basic element the oldest feeling we have
examined, a great love of the land, which, in addition to
its beauty, variety, and vast extent, had provided for
most of the inhabitants a well-being such as they could
not have enjoyed anywhere else.

Most colonists, without wholly realizing it, had developed or acquired certain characteristics and attitudes
common to all: a pride about their past and the distance
that many of them had come in life; a faith in their society and the capacity of their fellows collectively to reach
approved goals; the assurance that they could govern
themselves not just satisfactorily but well; and a belief in
a manifest destiny for themselves and their children. Certainly many people had been "merry in the Lord." "Happiness," said Saint-Just during the French Revolution, "is
a new thing in the world," but it was not new in
the American colonies. Thomas Jefferson substituted
"the pursuit of happiness" for the pursuit of "property"
in the great declaration not solely because of the felicity
of the phrase but because he knew full well that happiness was a singularly American trait, and a word given
wide currency by speakers and writers of the day.

The maturing colonial society, as Edmund Burke saw
so clearly, with its two millions of white people was
strong; those colonists given to reason pondered the doubling of their numbers every two or two-and-a-half
decades and were dazzled by the vistas and possibilities

such growth held out: their self-confidence shot up steadily and they felt a sense of power—growing power. Pride, though a cardinal sin in a godly people, was theirs also: they felt themselves to be more virtuous than the English; they imagined too that they were braver. In any event, time and the birthrate were on their side, and to bet on the future was uniquely American.

A feeling of unity evolved naturally out of these common characteristics and shared experiences, and it also gained strength from relationships that extended across provincial boundaries. Offspring had been numerous in this society composed dominantly of families that had roots in the soil going back, in some cases, from one to seven generations. Representatives of many families migrated to other colonies seeking new opportunities or more land. The Green family supplied Cambridge, Boston, New London, New Haven, Philadelphia, and Annapolis with skilled printers and several public figures. Five colonies contained members of the celebrated Franklin family, and in Connecticut, New York, and New Jersey were branches of the Hempstead family, and so it went. Another reason for changing residence was marriage. When Alice Lee of Westmoreland County married Dr. William Shippen and went to live in Philadelphia, she was the first of her family to reach out beyond the parochial limits of Virginia. Because so many South Carolinians, West Indians, and Philadelphia Quaker gentry summered at Newport after 1758, that resort became a veritable marriage mart for the colonial aristocracy. Berkeley Warm Springs and other spas on the Virginia frontier, Bristol and Yellow springs near Philadelphia, Stafford Springs and those at Bristol in Connecticut served a similar purpose for members of the middle class as well as for the better sort. In this way an unnoticed though highly important mingling took place that contributed to American rather than provincial viewpoints.

American patriotism had in it a very powerful religious element that was displayed in many different ways, but perhaps the one most effective was the concrete concern of the inhabitant for the welfare of his fellows whether they lived nearby or far off. Where the French idea of *Fraternité* was strongly abstract and secular, that of the colonists was more a humanitarian feeling born of Protestant teaching, leavened possibly by the common experience of growing up on a virgin continent. It was a kind of expansive sympathy, though lacking Wordsworth's overtones. The Puritan myth of the errand into the wilderness, which, as we have seen, Ezra Stiles broadened to "the errand into *America*," taught that God had urged His people to settle in the new Canaan, and had designated them a favored people. The confidence that God had never left them and would not abandon them as long as they kept the faith sustained them over and over again in the times that tried men's souls. If no patriot leader ever insisted that "God is American," the coins of the new United States would bear witness that "In God We Trust."

Reading the sources for the history of the years from 1760 through 1768, one quickly becomes aware of the accumulating evidence of patriotism and the increasing number of articulate expressions of this sentiment by all kinds of Americans. Anglican charges in 1763 that the early "dissenters" had been fanatics and purveyors of superstition were answered in the *Boston Gazette* by a writer who pointed out the ill-concealed contempt expressed by the missionaries of the S.P.G. for "the Fore-Fathers of this Country," who by this time were revered as champions of civil as well as ecclesiastical liberty. The rank and file of the readers of the *Gazette* would have concurred with the intensely patriotic declaration of John Adams at this time: "I have always considered the settlement of America with reverence and wonder, as the opening of a grand scheme and design in Providence for the illumination of the ignorant, and the emancipation of the slavish part of mankind all over the earth." [37]

The Reverend Noah Welles of Stamford preached the Connecticut Election Sermon on May 10, 1764, taking as his title *Patriotism Described and Recommended*. His text came from Luke: 7: 5: "For he loveth our nation, and he hath built us a synagogue." Welles equated true patriotism with public spirit or "a generous love to our country,—a regard for the happiness of our fellow-creatures." The firmest and unalterable basis for "public happiness" is liberty, and the parson insisted, wherever public spirit prevails, liberty is secure. He proceeded to explain in detail to his Hartford audience of legislators the kind of patriotism he was summoning them to exhibit:

"Further still; —love to our country requires us, that we act, as well as study and think, for the public good— The situation of our country may be such, as to demand the utmost exertion of our power and influence in its behalf: And the duty we owe the public, requires a chearful compliance with this demand. The true patriot is one, whose purse, as well as his heart, is open for the defense and support of his country. 'His liberal soul devises liberal things,' and his generous hand is ever ready to execute his liberal principles." For Noah Welles, "love to our country" was "universally incumbent upon every member of society," whatever his rank. [38]

For ardor and elegance in formulating American prin-

---

37. *Boston Gazette*, March 28, 1763; *Works of John Adams*, III, 452n.
38. Noah Welles, *Patriotism Described and Recommended* (New London, 1764), 5, 8, 12–13, 16, 29.

ciples, no one exceeded John Adams, whose second letter from the "Earl of Clarendon to John Pym" appeared in the *Boston Gazette* on January 20, 1766. "If ever an infant country deserved to be cherished it is America. If ever any people merited honor and happiness they are her inhabitants. They are a people whom no character can flatter or transmit in any expressions equal to their merit and virtue; with the high sentiments of Romans in the most prosperous and virtuous times of that commonwealth, they have the tender feelings of humanity and noble benevolence of Christians; they have the most habitual, radical sense of liberty, and the highest reverence for virtue; they are descended from a race of heroes, who, placing their confidence in Providence alone, set the seas and skies, monsters and savages, tyrants and devils, at defiance for the sake of religion and liberty.

"And the present generation have shown themselves worthy of their ancestors. Those cruel engines, fabricated by a British minister, for battering down all their rights and privileges, instead of breaking their courage and causing despondency, as might have been expected in their situation, have raised and spread through the whole continent a spirit that will be recorded to their honor with all future ages . . . The people, even to the lowest ranks, have become more attentive to their liberties, more inquisitive about them, and more determined to defend them, than they were ever before known, or had occasion to be. . . ." [39]

When Silas Downer solicited the Sons of Liberty of New York in 1766 to join in a union of similar groups throughout the colonies to be as watchmen on the walls for the protection of American liberties, he wrote a long and fervent letter explaining his plan, which concluded:

39. Adams, *Works*, III, 475–76.

"If, Gentlemen, I have been too free in my Sentiments, especially on the first corresponding, I hope you will impute it to an Enthusiasm in Liberty's Cause, which possessed my whole Soul in the later Controversies. My property is very small, but I have much Liberty, and I will die a Martyr to it before I will yield it." Though he does reveal "Enthusiasm," this is not bombast, for the Providence attorney was a level-headed thinker and writer, a skillful organizer, and a firm believer in America and things American. We know, moreover, that this letter accomplished his purpose. It was also Downer, who told the readers of the *Providence Gazette* (anonymously) on March 18, 1768: "Our Country is the finest of any in the whole World. It is the American Canaan." [40]

In the Quaker city at the rooms of the Union Library Company on January 1, 1768, Charles Thomson addressed his fellow members of the American Society, held at Philadelphia, for promoting Useful Knowledge. "Why should we hesitate to enlarge the plan of our Society, call to our Assistance Men of Learning and Ingenuity from every Quarter and unite in one generous, notable attempt not only to promote the Interest of our Country, but to raise her to some eminence in the rank of polite and learned nations?" Here, from the man who would soon be called the Sam Adams of Philadelphia, was a different brand of sentiment, what may be labeled cultural nationalism; and his proposal bore fruit within just one year in what is today the oldest learned body in the Western Hamisphere. [41]

The bitter and prolonged political-ecclesiastical struggle for power in New York, this same year, impelled

---

40. Downer to New York Sons of Liberty, July 21, 1766, in Bridenbaugh, *Silas Downer*, 94.
41. Junto Minutes, January 1, 1768 (Historical Society of Pennsylvania).

William Livingston to picture for his fellow men the future that Americans faced and to prophesy, with un-
canny accuracy, the precise time of their appointment
with destiny—1775: "Never had a nation such a prospect
as Britain of erecting a vast and durable empire. . . .
Courage, then Americans! liberty, religion, and sciences
are on the wing to these shores: the finger of God points
out a mighty empire to your sons."

"The day dawns in which the foundation of this
mighty empire is to be laid, by the establishment of a *regular American constitution*. All that has hitherto been done,
seems to be little besides the collection of materials, for
the construction of this glorious fabrick. 'Tis time to put
them together. The transfer of the European part of the
great family is so swift, and our growth so vast, that
before seven years [to 1775!], the first stone must be
laid.—Peace or war; famine or plenty; poverty or afflu-
ence; in a word no circumstance, whether prosperous or
adverse, can happen to our parent, nay, no possible
temper on her part, whether kind or cross grained, will
put a stop to this building. There is no contending with
Omnipotence, and the *predispositions* are so numerous,
and so well adapted to the rise of America, that our success is indubitable; and Britain, who began the work,
will not, cannot, withhold her assistance. Her assistance
did I say; She will spend all that she has.—nay, she is
coming, fast coming, in her own proper person, and will
desert her beloved island, to complete this stupendous
and lasting monument of her power. What an aera is this
to America! and how loud the call to vigilance, and activity! As we conduct, so it will fare with us and our children." [42]

In planning to make as much "noise and clamour" as

42. *New-York Gazette, or The Weekly Post-Boy*, April 11, 1768; reprinted in *A Collection of Tracts From the Late Newspapers . . .*
   (New York, 1768), I, 57–58.

possible against the Episcopalian dominance of New York in 1768, William Livingston remarked to Noah Welles that tracts and sermons were very helpful, but there was "greater Advantage in a weekly Paper, inserted in one of our Public Prints; which would be more generally read and reprinted." Governor Bernard showed that he was aware of this device when he dispatched copies of the "flagitious paper," the *Boston Gazette*, and the *Newport Mercury* to Secretary Pownall in 1765 "to Show how much bolder the Rhode Island printers are than ours." [43]

The newspapers also aided the patriot cause by making its new leaders better known everywhere. Possibly the most thorough "build-up" was provided John Dickinson, the lawyer of Philadelphia who wrote so many of the state papers of the Revolution. On November 5, 1767, the first of his twelve *Letters from a Farmer in Pennsylvania to the Inhabitants of the British Colonies* began to appear in the *Pennsylvania Chronicle*, and before the end of 1768, all but four newspapers had reprinted some or all of them. In addition they were published in book form in several cities and reached as many as three editions. [44]

The comings and goings of prominent colonials attracted the attention of the printers, who reported them, possibly as items of gossip, but the effect was to bring the men to the attention of the general public. A journey made by John Hancock of Boston to Philadelphia was followed by the Tory *Boston Chronicle*, which also paid close attention to the visit to Boston by several gentlemen of South Carolina. When Thomas Brattle and John Han-

---

43. Livingston to Welles, February 2, 1768, Johnson Family Papers, no. 86 (Yale University Library); Francis Bernard to Thomas Pownall, October 10, 1765, George Chalmers Papers relating to New England, I, 93, in Sparks MSS.

44. William Goddard stated in his *Pennsylvania Chronicle* on November 1, 1773, that there were 32 English language newspapers, two German, one English, and one French on this continent.

cock began their trip back, a Philadelphia gazette reported that "Their engaging Behavior added to their Firmness in the Cause of Liberty [and] rendered their Visit here very agreeable to all who had the pleasure of the Acquaintance." The following year when Henry Lloyd set out from Boston for New York, Philadelphia, and the southern provinces, the local press announced that all of his "Apparel and House Furniture" were of American manufacture, and everywhere he stopped along the route, the newspapers made careful note of these facts. Ralph Izard from Charleston and Thomas Mifflin of Philadelphia both visited Boston (later the New England court painter, John Singleton Copley made two of his most successful portraits of them and their wives).[45]

Probably no human phenomenon of the Western World in the eighteenth century is so worthy of note and speculation as the sudden appearance in the English colonies of a galaxy of statesmen and lesser political leaders seldom matched and never surpassed in history. Before 1760 politicians of greater than provincial stature were few; after that year they were almost legion. If, as many historians contend, the acid test of a nation is its capacity to produce leaders, then the Americans proved themselves a nation beyond all doubt. More than one Englishman and European perceived that for integrity, public spirit, talents, solidity of reasoning, literary style, and oratorical ability, the men who gathered at Philadelphia in the meetings of the continental congresses far outshone their opposite numbers at Westminster.

The events of the sixties and the burgeoning self-confidence of the people demonstrate that inside or outside of the British Empire the destiny of America seemed as-

45. *Boston Chronicle*, October 23, 30, 1769; March 26, 1770.

sured. The writings and speeches of prominent men echoed the sentiments of many Americans, particularly in the large seaports where many tradesmen and artisans held that the ills of the economy were directly attributable to the machinations of the authorities in the mother country. The colonies were now 150 years old, and they were strong—their strength had been tested in war and hard times, and as William Livingston had proclaimed, the "*predispositions* . . . are . . . so well adapted to the rise of America" that their success was indubitable.[46]

46. *New-York Gazette, or The Weekly Post-Boy*, April 11, 1768.

V
The Rising Glory of America
1770-1776

As the colonies passed the century-and-a-half mark, the divergence between them and the mother country became more apparent. One feature, which was an undoubted asset in the forming of a "public feeling" was observed in 1770 by an English visitor, William Eddis. In most English counties, the inhabitants spoke a distinct dialect and displayed habits and modes of thinking unique to themselves. To his surprise, Eddis discovered "in Maryland, and throughout the adjacent provinces . . . a striking similarity of speech universally prevails, and it is strictly true, that the pronunciation of the generality of the people has an accuracy and an elegance, that cannot fail of gratifying the most judicious ear." [1]

The colonials had been growing increasingly aware of the importance of speech in the field of communication. As early as 1762 Henry Miller began to print English lessons in his *Philadelphische Staatsbote* because the Germans and the English of Pennsylvania often misunderstood each other, and this proved a serious handicap in trade

1. William Eddis, *Letters from America* (London, 1792), 59, 60.

between them. In Boston "Spellarius" started giving interesting examples showing the divergence of American and British English and used the *Boston Gazette* to plead with "the Fraternity of Printers" for uniform spelling. In 1774, as a patriotic gesture, a Bostonian proposed in the first issue of the *Royal American Magazine* a plan for perfecting the English language on this continent "to the Literati of America." He wanted to establish "Fellows of the American Society of Language" who would publish each year studies and essays on improvements by which Americans would make "swifter advances to the summit of learning" than might be expected in the mother country. Despite endorsement by the printer of the *New Hampshire Gazette*, this laudable project never materialized, probably because of the political crisis. It is worthy of note, however, that years before independence had been declared, some men had an American language in mind, an idea that Noah Webster obviously drew upon when he started work in the seventeen eighties.[2]

The temper of the times also infected the colleges. In Princeton, Hugh Henry Brackenridge enlivened the commencement at Nassau Hall in 1771 by reading a patriotic epic, most of which had been written by a classmate, Philip Freneau. The performance won sufficient applause from the audience to warrant its prompt publication early in the next year in Philadelphia as *A Poem on the Rising Glory of America:*

> This is thy praise America . . .
>
> * * * *
>
> The seat of empire, the abode of kings,
> the final stage where time shall introduce
> Renowned characters, and glorious works

2. *Philadelphische Staatsbote*, July 5, 1762; *Boston Gazette*, March 4, 1765; *Royal American Magazine*, I (1774), 6–7; *New Hampshire Gazette*, April 22, 1774.

> Of high invention and of wond'rous art,
> which not the ravages of time shall waste
> Till he himself has run his long career.
>
>   *   *   *   *
>
>   . . . Paradise a new
> Shall flourish, by no second Adam lost." [3]

It was not, however, the efforts to improve the language nor the urging of Americans to rise to the "summit of learning" that aroused patriotic fervor as the new decade advanced. The seventies had brought no surcease from the strife and contention that plagued the mother country and her colonies. Instead, a series of crises resulting from the British attempt to coordinate and control the colonies further alienated the Americans, helped to consolidate public opinion, and finally drove them to open rebellion.

Genuine patriot doubts about the propriety and wisdom of the exasperated citizens of Providence in burning the revenue sloop *Gaspee* on June 9, 1772—an illegal destruction of government property—vanished quickly when news spread that the Ministry had ordered individuals charged with the act of vandalism to England for trial. This was a blunder on the part of Britain, and Americans had never reacted so strenuously. In delivering the Thanksgiving oration at the Second Baptist Church in Boston on December 3, the Reverend John Allen demonstrated the high pitch to which the public sense of outrage had risen in six months. In the affair no English laws had been broken. If there had been any transgression, he insisted, "the laws of America only are broke." For this "British Bostonian" not only denied the power of Parliament to legislate for and tax the colonies

---

3. [Philip Freneau and Hugh Henry Brackenridge], *A Poem on the Rising Glory of America, Being an Exercise Delivered at the Public Commencement at Nassau-Hall, September 25, 1772* (Philadelphia, 1772).

but also warned the Ministry in the person of the colonial secretary, Lord Dartmouth, that the Americans knew very well that all power originates in the people. "You know that the King of England has no right, according to the laws of GOD and nature, to claim the property of Americans without their consent. Liberty, my Lord, is the native right of the *Americans;* it is the blood-bought treasure of their Forefathers." [4]

Mr. Allen assumed that his listeners now unquestioningly accepted the position that William Livingston had taken in 1768 when he called for "an American Constitution." The minister summoned all colonists to establish and ensure their liberties, and also "that the *American* Parliament may enjoy every power and priviledge the *English* Parliament enjoy." In modern parlance, a power vacuum had developed on this side of the Atlantic, and he warned without equivocating, "where his Majesty has one soldier, America can produce fifty free men, and all volunteers; and raise a more potent army of men in three weeks, than Britain can in three years." [5]

In Virginia the threat to American liberties posed during the aftermath of the *Gaspee* affair led the House of Burgesses to initiate intercolonial legislative committees of correspondence, which promptly became an integral part of the movement for union so ardently urged by the newspaper press. The concept of two co-equal parliaments, one English and one American, had wide public support, for the idea behind it went all the way back to the revolutions of 1688–89. In effect it foretold the do-

4. John Allen, *An Oration, Upon the Beauties of Liberty, Or the Essential Rights*, 3d ed. (Boston, 1773), xvii–xviii. There were four editions of the *Oration* in Boston, and one each at Hartford, New London, and Wilmington, Del., in 1773.

5. Allen, *An Oration*, xxviii, 63. In 1773 the minister also published at Boston a similar work: *The American Alarm, Or The Bostonian Plea, For the Rights and Liberties of the People . . . By the British Bostonian.*

minion status worked out for Canada and the other British colonies in the nineteenth century

The campaign for union, which began in Virginia, received the endorsement of newspapers everywhere. In an essay "To the Americans" in the *Providence Gazette* in June 1773, "Sidney" wrote that: "the UNION of the Colonies, which is now taking Place, is big with the most important Advantages to this Continent. From the Union will result our Security from all foreign Enemies; for none will dare to invade us against the combined Force of these Colonies, nor will a British Parliament dare to attack our Liberties, when we are united to defend them. The united Americans may bid Defiance to all their open as well as secret Foes; therefore let it be the study of all to make the Union of the Colonies firm and perpetual, as it will be the great Basis for Liberty, and every public Blessing in America. In this Union every Colony will feel the Strength of the Whole; for if one is invaded, All will unite their Wisdom and Power in her Defence. In this Way the weakest will become strong, and America will soon be the Glory of the World, and the Terror of wicked Oppressors among the Nations. We cannot forbear triumphing in the Idea of the great Things, that will soon be accomplished in this Country, and the rapid Spread of American Glory.—But it is highly probable, that our most exalted Ideas fall far short of what will one Day be seen in America." [6]

The principal legal arguments against transporting any suspected *Gaspee* offenders to England for trial were drawn from *English Liberties, or the Free-Born Subject's Inheritance*, and because the fifth edition of 1721 was out of print, John Carter published a sixth containing some al-

6. *Providence Gazette*, June 12, 1773, and for a more fulsome statement that the Americans were the "most potent People that are lighted by the Sun," see issue of May 15, 1773.

terations "principally designed for America" on August 27, 1774. The list of subscribers at the end of the volume numbered 465, most of them inhabitants of Rhode Island, nearby Massachusetts, and Connecticut, who were willing to turn the rights and immunities of Britons to strictly American purposes.[7]

Samuel Johnson of Edenton, North Carolina, explained in September 1774 to a friend in England, where he himself had been born and reared, that he was so riveted to "America" by his connections that he could not "help feeling for it as if it were my *Natale Solum*." In his view, the British ministry had teased and fretted the people into rebellion ever since the passage of the Declaratory Act. After distinguishing sharply between America and Britain, he gave it as his opinion that "It is useless in disputes between different Countries, to talk about the right which one has to give Laws to the other." [8]

Despite his contempt for the common people of Massachusetts, young Captain William Evelyn with the British army at Boston correctly and succinctly defined the issue of the rebellion in a letter to his father, February 18, 1775. The Tories think that it was plotted by "a few ambitious, enterprising spirits," but "in my opinion the true causes of it are to be found in the nature of mankind; and [I think] that it proceeds from a new nation, feeling itself wealthy, populous, and strong; and being impatient of restraint, are struggling to throw off that dependency which is so irksome to them." [9]

7. *Providence Gazette*, November 7, 1772, September 18, 1773; August 27, 1774; and the *English Liberties* (350–56) for the subscribers' names.
8. *Colonial Records of North Carolina*, ed. William L. Saunders (Raleigh, 1890), IX, 1071.
9. *Letters of Captain W. Glanville Evelyn*, ed. G. D. Scull (Oxford, England, 1879), 46–47.

The times that produced great men also produced ordinary men of deep conviction and great courage, men ready to fight, perhaps to die, for their liberties. The unrest and democratic impulses so evident by 1773, impelled the Reverend Philip Reading, an Anglican missionary at Appoquinimink in the Lower Counties on the Delaware, to complain to the Secretary of the S. P. G. about "the relish which people have conceived for those ill-defined, misapprehended terms Liberty and Patriotism." Herein, as with so many of the Tories, he failed completely to fathom both the inhabitants as human beings and the spirit of the day.[10]

Benjamin Harrison was about to set out from his plantation and travel with Thomas Jefferson and Richard Henry Lee to Philadelphia to represent Virginia at the First Continental Congress in September 1774, when "a number of the plain people of the neighborhood waited on him and said, 'You assert there is a fixed intention to invade our rights and privileges; we own that we do not see this clearly, but since you assure us that it is so, we believe the fact.' They expressed their confidence that he would do what was right, and returned to their homes to abide the issue." This was not the first time—nor the last—that the good people of the Old Dominion unquestioningly followed trusted leaders without examining the issues.[11]

To the westward in the Great Valley of Virginia the Reverend Peter Muhlenberg faced his Lutheran congregation at Woodstock for the last time on a Sunday late in January 1776. Choosing a familiar text from Ecclesias-

10. *Historical Collections relating to the American Colonial Church*, ed. William S. Perry (New York, 1877), III, 463–64.
11. François Jean, Marquis de Chastellux, *Travels in North America in the Years 1780–1781–1782* (New York, 1827), 277.

tes 3: 1–8: "To every thing there is a season, and a time
. . . a time of war, and a time of peace," the minister,
who was also a community leader and had served Dun-
more County in the House of Burgesses, explained to his
German flock precisely what was at stake for all Americans. At the close of the service, dramatically he shed his
clerical gown and stood before them in the uniform of a
colonel of the Virginia militia. Shortly thereafter, the
former pastor raised and assumed command of the 8th
Virginia Regiment, which was composed largely of Germans from the settlements along the Shenandoah.[12]

The average New England Yankee had been raised in
town meetings and had heard from countless sermons
about his rights and liberties. Lieutenant Joseph Hodgkins of the Ipswich Minute Men went off to Bunker Hill
at the age of thirty-two. On March 20, 1776, he wrote
from Camp Prospect Hill at Cambridge to his wife: "you
whare full of trouble for fear that I should be Called
away. I would not have you Be uneasy about me, for I
am willing to sarve my Contery in the best way and
manner that I am Capeble of, and as our Enemy are gone
from us I Expect we must follow them. It is not sarting
yet who will stay hear, But it is generaly thought that
our Reg[imen]t will March some where. I would not Be
understood that I should Chuse to March, But as I am
engaged in this glories Cause I am will[ing] to go whare I
am Called with a desire to Commit myself and you to the
care of him Who is able to Carry on through all the
Defi[cul]ties . . . I am sensible that the feteagues of
marching will Be grate, But I hope if we are Called to it,
we shall March with Chearfulness." [13]

12. Paul A. W. Wallace examines the several versions of this incident
    critically in *The Muhlenbergs of Pennsylvania* (Philadelphia, 1950),
    116–19; see also, *Dictionary of American Biography*, XIII, 312.
13. An excellent example of the printed patriotic sermons that Joseph

In 1798, William Manning, a farmer and an early Jeffersonian democrat dwelling in the midst of high Federalists at North Billerica, ruminated over the events of twenty-three years before. He was a man of no great learning, had never traveled more than sixty miles from home, and was no great reader of books. "But I always thought it my duty to search into and see for my selfe in all maters that consansed me as a member of society, and when the war began between Brittain and Amarica I was in the prime of Life and highly taken up with Liberty and a free Government . . . But I believed then and still believ it is a goode cause which we aught to defend to the very last, and I have bin a constant Reader of publick Newspapers and have closely attended to men and measures ever sence." [14]

These two Yankees resembled those of Connecticut of whom a royal customs official reported in 1772: "They are all Politicians, and all Scripture learnt." More sophisticated in some ways, though not much more traveled, was Brigadier General Nathanael Greene, who very quickly divested himself of any Rhode Island provincialism that he might once have had. From the outbreak of the conflict he placed great stress on "the General Interest," and on June 23, 1775, he wrote incisively to Governor Nicholas Cooke: "I hope the little Colony of Rhode Island . . . wont be the first to oppose the measures of the Continental Congress, the united council and

Hodgkins and other Yankees were reading was a tract of sixty-six pages by Amos Adams, published at Boston in 1769: *A Concise, Historical View of the Perils, Hardships, Difficulties and Discouragements which have attended the planting and progressive improvements of New-England; with a particular account of its long and destructive wars, expensive expeditions . . . In two Discourses. This Glorious Cause,* ed. Herbert T. Wade and Robert A. Lively (Princeton, 1958), 195. Punctuated slightly for clarity.

14. William Manning, *The Key of Libberty,* ed. Samuel Eliot Morison (Billerica, Mass., 1922), 3.

strength of America. We are but as the drop of [*sic*] a bucket." [15]

The events that followed inexorably are known to everyone. At the First Continental Congress, Joseph Galloway's statesmanlike proposal for an American parliament failed by one vote; it came too late. In its place the Association was created as a coercive commercial weapon to be used against the mother country, which was overt rebellion. The following April, blood was shed at Lexington and Concord, and armed revolt inevitably led to independence.[16]

The Spirit of '76 was far from being new or novel when independence from Great Britain was officially declared on July 2, 1776. A deeply felt love of America and a sensible realization of the bonds of unity far surpassing provincial boundaries had been developing slowly and silently over the long stretch of time since the establishing of the first English settlement at Jamestown. In every way the Spirit of '76 was the culmination of the 169 years that compose nearly all of the first half of our history.

15. Ann Hulton, *Memoirs of a Loyalist Lady* (Cambridge, 1927), 105; Nathanael Greene to Governor Nicholas Cooke, June 23, 1775, Papers of Nathanael Greene (MSS, Rhode Island Historical Society).

16. The Continental Association provided that all colonies would cease to import from and export to Britain, Ireland, and the West Indies. Significantly, it authorized the setting up of extralegal machinery to enforce the agreement. Radical though the Association was, it did not satisfy the ardent John Adams, who on July 17, 1774, wrote to James Warren about the approaching meeting at Philadelphia: ". . . What avails, Prudence, Wisdom, Policy, Fortitude, Integrity, without Power, without Legions? When Demosthenes, (God forgive the Vanity of recollecting his Example) went Ambassador from Athens to the other States of Greece, to excite a Confederacy against Philip, he did not go to propose a Non-Importation or Non-Consumption Agreement!!!" *Warren-Adams Letters*, I, 29, Massachusetts Historical Society, *Collections*, LII (1917).

In the light of this long course of growth and expansion the meetings of the First and the Second Continental congresses no longer appear as inexplicable and cataclysmic events. The roots of these sentiments and the emotions of pride and resentment, the great fear of approaching tyranny that suddenly burst forth during the fifteen years before the First Congress convened in Philadelphia had been planted early in the seventeenth century and had been growing slowly but steadily thereafter, unmentioned and almost unnoticed until about 1739. "Indeed," as John Dickinson so cogently put it, "nations, in general, are not apt to *think* until they *feel*." [17]

A few astute persons, sensing the changes brought about by the religious revolution and open warfare, began to think and reason, to examine the true nature of the connection of the colonies with the mother country. In time men of all classes and conditions suspected that the religious liberties and self-government that they enjoyed were being seriously threatened by what they judged to be a plot to effect a thorough-going reordering of the empire. In defense, they argued hard against Parliamentary power, admitting only allegiance to the monarch. When their insistence that they be admitted to what is known today as "dominion status" was ignored and naked force was used against Massachusetts, they took up arms.

Throughout the century and a half of growing American unity, both the religious and political institutions of the colonists became ever more republican in nature. Not more than a handful of Americans had ever laid eyes on the king, and the very feeling of being under a monarch was truly alien to "this fierce people," as Edmund Burke described them. Liberty they understood, for they had experienced more of it than any other people in the

17. John Dickinson, *Letters from a Farmer in Pennsylvania* (Philadelphia, 1768), no. XI, p. 59.

world, and the "unquestionable republicanism of the American mind," having long ago rejected monarchy in the church, in the sixties and seventies discovered that it had grown politically repugnant as well. No reader familiar with the history of these years should marvel that Thomas Jefferson directed the bill of particulars against the king in his great declaration. From Silas Downer's first statement of 1768 right down to the resolves of the First Continental Congress in 1774, the colonial constitutional position had been elucidated publicly with notable clarity: the colonies were bound to the British Empire solely by their allegiance to the king, and from him, therefore, they had to separate in 1776.

Something more than a majority of the people—many of them rapidly and positively, others slowly—underwent what the French call *un bouleversement intellectuel* after 1760. Denied co-equal status with all other Englishmen, whether in Britain or in the dominions, they determined to go it alone as a new country in the family of nations. First they moved to armed rebellion and then to declaring independence, because a majority of them became convinced that theirs was a better country than what Benjamin Franklin was now calling a "rotten old State." For them America was riding the wave of the future. The many serious difficulties the new nation experienced in struggling to attain unified political action—making thirteen clocks strike in unison, as John Adams put it so well—did not preclude ultimate success, which was possible because the people entertained common emotional and rational sentiments about nearly all other aspects of life, sentiments they had held for more than 169 years.

Undeniably there was a substantial minority in the population that opposed armed resistance to Britain, and among the patriots themselves good Americans and true could not go the whole way to independence. John Dickinson was one of the latter group; he resigned from Congress rather than vote for independence. But once the decision was made, he entered the army and fought for what he could not vote for.

It is striking that many of the ablest Tories who went into exile voluntarily later became disillusioned with Britain and the British. Like Samuel Sewall in the sixteen-nineties, they felt like strangers in the land. Samuel Curwen and Peter van Schaack went back home again to Salem and Kinderhook; Thomas Hutchinson died in England, homesick for Milton Hill. Then there were men who straddled the fence like Ashley Bowen of Marblehead: he "never could perceive the path which she [America] could move to marine power" and remained firm in his faith in "the omnipotence of the British navy," retaining a "sacred attachment to British everything, Navy, Church, State." Nevertheless "his country was dear to him" and despite his views, this fifth-generation American chose to live out his days in America. Late in 1776, Admiral Lord Howe startled his secretary, Ambrose Serle, with the comment that "almost all the People of Parts and Spirit were in the Rebellion." To the leaders and the hosts of simple followers, "this glories Cause" was being waged to ensure the future of the America they loved.[18]

John Adams knew all about the aspirations, beliefs, and convictions of his fellow colonials from observation and experience, which in after years he reinforced by profound reflection upon men and events. This master of all students of the era concluded in 1818 in a letter to

18. *The Journals of Ashley Bowen*, Colonial Society of Massachusetts, *Publications*, XLV (Boston, 1973), II, 624-25; *The American Journal of Ambrose Serle*, ed. George B. Tatum (San Marino, Calif., 1940), 157.

Hezekiah Niles: "The Revolution was in the minds and hearts of the people; a change in their religious sentiments of their duties and obligations. This radical change in the principles, opinions, sentiments, and the affections of the people, was the real American Revolution." [19]

The real American Revolution and the Spirit of '76 were one and the same thing, and there was nothing new about them—they had a long lineage of 169 years.

19. *The Works of John Adams*, ed. Charles Francis Adams (Boston, 1854), X, 282–83, 288, 313.

Index